Online Freelancing Mastery

The Ultimate Guide to Making Money as a Freelancer—Unlock Proven Strategies to Monetize Your Skills and Talents, Attract Clients, and Build a Thriving Freelance Business

Change Your Life Guru

Books by **Change Your Life Guru**:

Affiliate Marketing Mastery: *The Ultimate Guide to Starting Your Online Business and Earning Passive Income - Unlock Profitable Affiliate Secrets, Boost Earnings with Expert Strategies, Top Niches, High-Performance Products, Innovative Tactics and Essential Tools for Success*

Dropshipping Business Mastery: *The Ultimate Guide to Starting & Managing a Thriving Dropshipping Business - Skyrocket Your Income with Proven Strategies, Profitable Niches, and Unleash Powerful Marketing Tactics*

Etsy Store Mastery: *The Ultimate Guide to Building Your Own Etsy Empire - Learn Proven Strategies for Finding & Selling the Hottest Products, Building Your Brand, and Dominating Your Niche on Etsy*

Online Course Mastery: *The Ultimate Guide to Creating and Marketing Profitable Online Courses - Learn How to Find Your Niche, Create Engaging Content, and Succeed as an Online Course Creator*

Online Freelancing Mastery: *The Ultimate Guide to Making Money as an Online Freelancer - Unlock Proven Strategies to Monetize Your Skills and Talents, Market Yourself, and Go from Zero To Success*

Online Tutoring: *The Ultimate Guide to Creating a Profitable Online Tutoring Business – Become an Expert in Your Niche, Craft Engaging Sessions, Harness Powerful Marketing Strategies, and Profit from Your Expertise in the Digital Learning World*

Print on Demand Mastery: *The Ultimate Blueprint for Print on Demand Success - Unlock Actionable Tips & Strategies to Starting, Setting Up, and Marketing a Profitable Print on Demand Business*

Social Media Influencer: *The Ultimate Guide to Building a Profitable Social Media Influencer Career - Learn How to Build Your Brand, Create Viral Content, and Make Brands Beg to Pay for Your Lifestyle*

Subscription Business Model: *The Ultimate Guide to Building and Scaling A Predictable Recurring Income Business - Attract and Retain Loyal Subscribers, and Maximize Your Profitability with Proven Strategies and Best Practices*

YouTube Influencer: *The Ultimate Guide to YouTube Success, Content Creation, and Monetization Strategies - Build and Grow a Thriving YouTube Channel and Boost Engagement with Proven Techniques and Insider Secrets*

THANK YOU – A Gift For You!

THANK YOU for purchasing our book! *You could have chosen from dozens of other books on the same topic but you took a chance and chose this one.* As a token of our appreciation, we would like to offer you an exclusive **FREE GIFT BOX**. Your Gift Box contains powerful downloadable products, resources and tools that are the perfect companion to your newly-acquired book, and are designed to catapult you towards freedom and success.

To get instant access, just go to: https://changeyourlife.guru/toolkit

Inside your Free Gift Box, you'll receive:

- **Goal Planners and Schedulers**: Map out manageable and actionable steps so you have clarity and are empowered with a clear roadmap to achieve every goal.

- **Expert Tips & Tricks:** Invaluable tips and strategies ready to apply to your life, or business, to accelerate your progress and reach your outcomes.
- **Exclusive Content:** Free bonus materials, resources, and tools to help you succeed.
- **New Freebies:** Enter your email address to download your free gift box and be updated when we add new Free Content, ensuring you always have the tools, information and strategies to sky-rocket your success!

Are you ready to supercharge your life? Download your gift box for FREE today! [**https://changeyourlife.guru/toolkit**]

Table of Contents

INTRODUCTION **1**

- BENEFITS 5
  - *Unlimited Earning Potential* *5*
  - *Autonomy* *6*
  - *Less Distractions* *6*
  - *Location* *7*
  - *Constructive Partnerships* *7*
  - *Commute* *8*
- DISADVANTAGES 8
  - *Benefits* *8*
  - *Unsteady Income* *9*
  - *Isolation* *9*
  - *Unpaid work* *10*
- A GLIMPSE INTO FREELANCING 12

CHAPTER 1: FINDING YOUR FREELANCE NICHE **15**

- SWIMMING WITH THE CURRENT 17
- LOOKING INWARD 19
  1. *The Best or One of the Best* *20*
  2. *The Early Stages* *22*
  3. *The 30-Day Experiment* *23*
- DEFINING YOUR USP 24
- DO NOT PREEMPTIVELY QUIT YOUR JOB 28
- LEARN HOW TO NEGOTIATE WITH CLIENTS 29
- MASTER YOUR ON-BOARDING 30
- CHECKLIST 31

CHAPTER 2: IDENTIFYING YOUR TARGET MARKET **33**

- RESEARCH 34
- THE IDEAL TARGET MARKET 35
- FOUR QUESTIONS TO CONSIDER 36
- CHECKLIST 42

CHAPTER 3: NAVIGATING FREELANCE PLATFORMS **43**

- FREELANCING PLATFORMS VS. JOB BOARDS 44
- FREELANCE PLATFORMS 45
  - *Brand vs. Person* *45*
  - *Streamlined Interactions* *46*

Support *47*
Portfolio *47*
JOB BOARDS 48
Payment Fee *48*
Communication *49*
SO, WHICH IS BETTER? 50
TOO MUCH TOO SOON 51
FINDING THE RIGHT PLATFORM 53
Pricing Model *53*
Target Platform *54*
Upwork *54*
Fiverr *55*
LinkedIn *55*
CHECKLIST 57

CHAPTER 4: MANAGING CLIENT RELATIONSHIPS 59

THREE REASONS WHY CLIENT RELATIONSHIPS ARE IMPORTANT 61
E-Commerce *61*
Less Client Attrition *61*
"Word of Mouth" Marketing *62*
BECOMING A CLIENT PROJECT MANAGER 63
9 TIPS ON ENSURING EFFECTIVE CLIENT RELATIONSHIPS 64
Communicate Effectively *64*
Keep Things Positive *66*
Keep an Open Mind *67*
Don't Lose Sight of the Human Factor *68*
Learn to Anticipate Their Ideas and Needs by Getting to Know Them *69*
Go Above and Beyond Their Expectations of You and the Project *72*
Set and Enforce Clear Boundaries *73*
Assert Yourself as the Unrivaled Expert *74*
Give Yourself and Ask For Feedback *76*
CHECKLIST 78

CHAPTER 5: MARKETING YOURSELF AS AN ONLINE FREELANCER 79

MARKETING STRUGGLES 80
Imposter Syndrome *80*
Time Management *82*
Lack of Knowledge *82*
MARKETING STRATEGIES 83
Personal Network *83*
LinkedIn *84*
Have an Online Portfolio *85*

Use Social Media Strategically *88*
Guest Blogging *89*
Customized Services *90*
Always Ask for Reviews and Recommendations *90*
Checklist 93

CHAPTER 6: THE SUCCESS-ORIENTED MINDSET OF AN ONLINE FREELANCER 95

The Importance of Having a Success-Oriented Mindset 96
How to Create a Success-Oriented Mindset 97
Understanding Your Priorities *97*
Goal-Setting *98*
The Power of Positive Thinking *99*
Take a Break *100*
Create a Routine *101*
Staying Motivated *102*
Seek Guidance *104*
Don't Compare *105*
Keep an Open Mind *105*
The Neuroscience of a Success-Oriented Mindset 106
Checklist 108

CHAPTER 7: CONTINUING PROFESSIONAL DEVELOPMENT 109

What Is Continuing Professional Development (CPD)? 109
Upskilling 112
Reskilling 113
Benefits of CPD for Freelancers 114
Setting Up Your CPD Initiatives 116
Checklist 117

CHAPTER 8: WHAT I HAVE LEARNED AS AN ONLINE FREELANCER 119

8 Things I Learned From Working as an Online Freelancer 120
Personal Branding *120*
Be Unique *121*
Mindset *122*
Braving the Unknown *123*
Just Do It *124*
Balance Is an Illusion *125*
Ensure You Have a Financial Buffer *126*
Practice Quality vs. Quantity When It Comes to Clients *127*
Checklist 129

CONCLUSION 131

Summary: The Importance of Taking a Break....................135
Summary: The Importance of Having a Work Plan....................136
Summary: The Importance of Client Interactions....................138
Summary: The Importance of Picking the Right Platform....................140
The Importance of Getting Started....................143

Introduction

If you are not willing to risk the unusual, you will have to settle for the ordinary. – Jim Rohn.

Why has the idea of becoming a freelancer been rising in popularity in recent years? Is it because the pandemic made remote workers out of all of us and urged many employees to demand the best out of their own creativity and ingenuity when searching for ways to generate income during lockdown? Is the proposition of being your own boss and managing your own projects and schedule so attractive that it leads to people seeking secondary forms of passive income, or in some cases, leaving their full-time jobs altogether to pursue a life in freelancing?

The truth lies somewhere in between these reasons mentioned above and more. Another undeniable truth is that although many people have a superficial understanding of what freelancing entails, most are unaware of what is truly required to make freelancing a viable and financially sound way of living, especially in the current market where more and more businesses are outsourcing their duties to freelancers.

Another essential consideration to bear in mind when contemplating venturing into freelancing is the amount of work required to get started and consequently maintain your business afloat once you get some traction and have a steady stream of work and clients.

Still, the vision of a person sitting by themselves in a quaint and cozy café, working away on a small laptop nicely nestled on their lap while working away on their third coffee can make anyone currently stuck in traffic or in between other packed-in rush hour passengers flirt with the idea of becoming a freelancer. Despite the hard work and many moving parts that need to be skillfully managed to become a successful freelancer—success being defined as making enough money to sustain yourself and your dependents—freelancing is like any other professional endeavor in that the outcome depends on what you make of it. Enter freelancing prepared and knowledgeable about what awaits you. You will be able to secure your independence and enjoy the many benefits of not being a nine-to-five employee.

Any skilled and disciplined person can embrace and thrive from freelancing. One of the most crucial things differentiating those who will succeed as freelancers and those who don't—or those who have a more challenging time trying to make it work—is preparedness.

As a business employee, the employer manages a significant portion of what is required to integrate yourself into a company successfully. Onboarding can be as simple as spending a day being guided around a new building, being introduced to your new colleagues, and being trained on how to perform your new job effectively. As a freelancer, you will not have this luxury.

Freelancers are the masters of their domain, or at least they should be, which is why they are often referred to as solopreneurs. Freelancers differ from entrepreneurs in that freelancers do not run a business consisting of employees who require monthly wages or benefits such as medical, but act as every department of their business, from HR to Marketing, and are the sole business entity of their enterprise. In other words, the brand they are building is solely based on their particular skills and talents and how those can be leveraged to offer products and services to third parties.

Therefore, getting started as a freelancer is one of the most challenging aspects of this lifestyle. Unlike when you are onboarded as a new employee, getting started as a freelancer requires you to manage and attend to every facet of the new business you are creating. You can always ask for help from knowledgeable and skilled people, but at the end of the day, the final decision regarding your business will always come down to you.

Unfortunately, there is no training seminar or performance review from your superior to let you know how you are doing and what you should be doing moving forward to be more productive at your job. Everything from planning to execution and analysis is entirely in your hands. Freelancers are not only responsible for generating enough work to keep them busy and earning sufficient income, but they must also be constantly working at growing the business and the brand.

Some people prefer this hands-on, autonomous approach, while others can find it intimidating. Regardless of how you feel, it is imperative that you educate yourself on the right ways to start freelancing so that you can turn it into a sustainable long-term profession.

Knowing how to avoid the pitfalls and leverage the right opportunities can help you side-step or better handle the adversities that come to any person trying to make a life for themselves by freelancing.

In a sense, this book is a guide on how to master the discipline of self-accountability and perseverance. The book also details how to convert your skills into competencies that clients and businesses will find enticing and pay you to implement into their business model. Moreover, by reading this book, you will learn how to recognize and hone your skills and market those skills as a lucrative brand that portrays confidence and mastery.

Regardless of what specific industry, niche, or discipline you are leveraging to become a freelancer, the universal truth that binds all freelance writers, graphic designers, marketers, etc., is that preparation is key.

Just like you would not walk into a job interview without having done your homework, you should not venture into a life of freelancing without having undergone the necessary research. Even if you are aiming to conduct freelancing work as a side gig, you will miss out on many gainful opportunities if you are not aware of how to portray and conduct yourself as a freelancer and how to make the shift from being a nine-to-five employee to becoming a solopreneur who is in charge of every area of their business.

Therefore, I have condensed into this guide the most fruitful and imperative considerations you must have as you begin your journey into freelancing. Furthermore, this book will steer you through the challenges you will face when trying to time manage all your different responsibilities. Finally, once you have finished reading the entire book, you will be left with a sound plan of action and a comprehensive list of valuable resources that you will always have at your disposal. These resources are specifically tailored for the modern freelancer looking to ensure their freedom while converting their ideas and creative vision into a thriving business that you can manage while having that third cup of coffee while sitting at your favorite café or on a plane to your favorite summer destination.

Before getting started, it is important to provide context to the notion of pursuing a life in freelancing. Perhaps you are wondering, how many freelancers are there in the world? How has this business model evolved over time? What type of work can be converted into a freelancing service? The truth is, freelancing has never been more popular, and there has never been a better time to aspire to become a solopreneur.

According to a recent study, more than a third of the U.S. workforce is conducting freelancing work in some capacity, either as their sole source of income or as a second job. The pandemic forced many people to look inwards to find ways to make income using the internet and their skills. Those with creative flair began offering their unique talents as services to the businesses that were still operating during this time and found that since the demand was low, they could actually turn their pandemic projects into a stable source of revenue.

The internet became one of the most valuable assets during this time, so most communication happened online, giving more spotlight to freelancers trying to market their businesses.

Interestingly, freelancing has been evolving even before the pandemic and is expected to continue growing at an even more exponential rate. In 2014, around 53 million people were working as freelancers in America. Last year in 2022, there were around 70.4 million, meaning freelancing grew by 33% in just six years, which is an astounding figure. Perhaps more striking, however, is the prediction that this industry is set to continue growing by 168% over the next ten years.

These stats should put in perspective for you how freelancing is no gimmick or alternative to hard work, but, in fact, a very viable career choice. However, with the rising popularity comes an increase in competition, especially in content writing, which is currently the most popular mode of freelancing work. Competition is not necessarily bad, as it inherently requires the quality of freelancing work to be elevated and brings more awareness to the benefits of freelancers as an integral part of people's businesses. However, the reality is that the rise in popularity of freelancing means that aspiring solopreneurs must scrutinize and review the current freelancing market to understand what components of this industry is driving it forward and what the challenges are that make others fall short and become thwarted by competitors.

Although this book will provide practical success factors that every person can integrate into their business strategy, the first thing every aspiring freelancer must do before embarking on their solo career is define the purpose and reason behind their decision to pursue freelancing professionally.

Imagine six months into chasing your dreams of being your boss and managing your own hours when you are suddenly faced with the reality of what you are getting yourself into. Sometimes the surprise factor is enough to discourage some from abandoning freelancing altogether, even if it ultimately is something that would bring them a lot of joy and freedom.

To avoid this happening, let us delve into the realities of a life of freelancing, complete with benefits and disadvantages.

Benefits

Unlimited Earning Potential

One of the most sought-after advantages of freelancing, but one that perhaps people do not consider when first contemplating this career path is the fact that there is no limit to how much they can make as income. When considering a life in freelancing, people tend to focus on the early stages of what this career path entails and become disheartened by the notion that they will not be making as much money as they were when working as full-time employees. Although this will most likely be the case for most budding freelancers, it is also important to consider what your circumstance will look like a few years down the line if you execute your freelancing career successfully. The truth is that there is no limit to how much you can earn in a given year other than your potential to retain and acquire new clients. If you persevere with a sound strategy, you can double and even triple your previous salary; in other words, there is no boss or contract in the way of you earning exactly what you deserve and what you put into each project.

Autonomy

Let's be honest, it's a very enticing proposition to not have a boss or any direct superior to report to in your line of work. This proposition is exactly the work environment you will be met with as a freelancer. The only person you will have to report to is yourself, as you are in charge of every facet of your business. You will not have to execute strategies that you do not agree with and consider to be harmful to the business, or face an angered tirade whenever you make a mistake. Knowing that the actions you undertake related to your work come with genuine conviction will add to the motivation you feel to execute them to your utmost ability.

Less Distractions

No one likes office politics, and as entertaining as workplace drama can sometimes be—as long as it does not involve you directly—it is nevertheless a distraction from your work. This is not to say that freelancers are unaffected by distractions, but they possess the ability to do away with external influences that can deter them from focusing on their work in a way that is not feasible in an office. Sometimes the distraction can be something as simple as a thought. Employees can often find themselves immersed in thoughts regarding competitiveness with other coworkers and frustration when a colleague attempts to thwart their success or undermines their efforts. Being in such close proximity to the same people day in and day out creates the risk of distraction which does not exist in the working life of a freelancer. Naturally, there will still be distractions in the form of errands and personal appointments, but these are still under your control and how you manage these distractions is still under your control.

Location

Just like in real estate, we must stress the importance of location, location, location, when it comes to examining the benefits of being a solopreneur. Even if the office you worked in during your time as a full-time employee was as lavish and commodious as can be, undergoing the grueling endeavor that is rush-hour traffic every weekday is enough to dishearten even the most motivated of people. Furthermore, working in the same space every week gets tiresome quite quickly. Freelancing allows you to decide where you work, based on preference and convenience. As I alluded to earlier, you have the freedom to sit in your favorite coffee shop and work, surrounded by other creative individuals who have chosen to pursue the same career path, or work from home if you feel that you must be as time efficient as possible.

Constructive Partnerships

Considering that freelancing requires you to be constantly communicating with clients, either prospective or existing, it is important that you feel comfortable with those working relationships. As a nine-to-five employee, you do not have the ability to decide which people you work with and which you don't. This does not exclusively apply to clients. At work, you might be put in a team where one or more people within that team you do not work well with. As a freelancer, you have the privilege of deciding which business to take on and which not to, and you are not beholden to being around the same group of people day in and day out.

Commute

As mentioned previously, freelancers can work from wherever they can find a stable wifi connection and a place to sit and place their laptop on. Some freelancers prefer to work from home, and others like to be surrounded by others while they work, it depends entirely on the individual. The important consideration is that it is their choice. Having to get up at the same time every morning to go through the stress of trying to get to work on time can put a damper on how your morning gets started. Furthermore, this daily ritual has the tendency to create a significant dent in your expenses. By not being bound to a schedule, you can save a lot of money and time. What you make with the added time and money is entirely up to you, but as a freelancer, it is important that you learn not to waste any of it and always leverage it to your advantage.

If this is all beginning to sound like a very rewarding and enticing proposition, it's because if done right, freelancing has the power to produce many benefits in your life, which you will be able to enjoy with the added freedom you have secured for yourself.

As attractive as this lifestyle may seem, there are nevertheless some disadvantages that must be mentioned, so you receive a full understanding of what freelancing entails.

Disadvantages

Benefits

No, this does not refer to a benefit that freelancing offers, the opposite, in fact. Unlike their nine-to-five counterparts, freelancers do not receive any of the corporate benefits that most companies give to their employees, such as health insurance, medical, paid holidays, and sick days. Of course, there are ways where freelancers can create these opportunities for themselves, but they lose the privilege of having a third party organize and manage these benefits for them, the most notable example probably being taxes. When working as a freelancer, you must exercise the autonomy you have secured for yourself professionally in the way you manage your taxes.

Unsteady Income

While it is true that freelancers have an unlimited earning potential that is solely reliant on their effort output, sometimes that potential can be quite minimal, especially when first starting out on this venture. As a new freelancer, you will spend the majority of your first months, or even years, just getting your brand and business strategy set up. You will not yet have a vast portfolio or projects and clients that you can show people that are looking for someone to manage their business, so you will have to do a lot of field marketing to get your name out there. As frustrating as it can sometimes be to not be generating any income at the beginning, this is a completely normal occurrence that you must exercise with patience and determination.

However, even experienced freelancers can go through rough patches where they either lose clients or fail to acquire more, leading them to not be able to expand and continue to grow their business, which should always be the focus of any freelancer.

There is also the consideration that just the very uncertainty of not knowing how much you are going to make in a given year is enough to make a freelancer anxious, even if they are doing well and have secured financial freedom. Some might view this situation as a lack of stability, while others see it as an opportunity to feel challenged and motivated to work harder.

Isolation

Being a freelancer can be a lonely occupation at times. Even if you are in constant communication with other people around the world as you try to make your business thrive, at the end of the day you will most likely never be able to replicate the same workplace environment that you would be inhabiting if you were an employee. This consideration is also very dependent on personality. There are some individuals, perhaps the more introverted ones, who might relish at the fact that their business interactions will all mostly be handled online. However, there are others who might feel isolated and lonely, and might miss the opportunity to head to the water cooler for a short break to talk about the weekend with a colleague.

Unpaid work

This is not necessarily much of a disadvantage unless you need money urgently. Still, much of the work that a freelancer does to keep their business afloat is called non billable work. One of the fundamentals components of successful freelancing is marketing. As a freelancer, you cannot delegate any social media strategies to your marketing department because you are that department, and unfortunately you are not getting paid for the work you produce. Having a social media presence is imperative nowadays, so it is important that you are as active as possible online to get your name out there and in the minds of prospective clients. While you will not be immediately monetarily compensated for your marketing strategy, you are sure to see the rewards of these efforts as time passes and people start scrolling and noticing your brand.

Every one of these considerations are situations that can be expanded upon or mitigated to create the most practical working conditions for yourself. By being creative and focusing on your overriding goal, you will surely find ways to make whatever disadvantage you might initially find when getting started with freelancing into a success factor. This fact is especially poignant when it comes to the non billable work consideration. While generating income is a valid and necessary priority for anyone, freelancing will require that you exercise self-confidence and resilience, things that will serve you well for the rest of your life.

Having a clear and well thought out goal is imperative to freelancing success, so much so that it is the first step every aspiring freelancer must take when starting out. Without a goal, you will struggle to find the motivation and focus needed to push through adversity and uncertainty.

Your goal does not have to be overly-elaborate or aspirational; if you simply want to find a way to generate some added passive income to your life, that is a completely acceptable goal. The most important thing you must do is be honest with yourself.

Once you have put forth an achievable and desirable goal for yourself, look into how you want your financial situation to look like. If you are doing freelancing on the side and continue to work a nine to five job, figure out how much time you can devote to freelancing and what are the best times for you to focus exclusively on your side hustle so that your freelancing venture receives the attention it deserves. If you decide to go all-in, and leave your full-time job to pursue freelancing, be very analytical about calculating how much money you will need to make each month to cover your living expenses, and possibly those of your dependents.

The next step in your freelance preparations is equally as important as defining a tangible and realistic goal. An irrefutable fact when it comes to freelancing is that less is more when it comes to defining a niche, or a specific market you want to tap into with your products or services; this is something we will delve deep into in the first chapter.

The way people do business in the modern world is changing. Individuals are discovering and devising new and innovative ways to craft their own opportunities and sources of revenue. Young and old people alike are learning to harness their talents on a global scale to create content, provide technical solutions, or counsel businesses on their finances or accounting, to name only a few of the ways freelancing can forge a sustainable way of life.

With the rise in popularity of freelancing work, for both the freelancers and the clients using this service for their businesses, never has there been more information and opportunity available for those seeking to secure their freedom while creating a profitable way of living.

There is a lot of information to cover, but all of it will ensure that you are fully prepared to take the right first steps into a new lifestyle that has the potential to give you a life worth dreaming about.

There are aspects to freelancing that make this venture something unlike any other professional endeavor, which requires people to adjust their mindset and their routines. Freelancing requires that people give their best efforts to address their many different responsibilities all at once, which requires a person to think like a CEO but act like an employee working as hard as they can to rise through the professional ranks of a company.

Although you will not be managing any subordinates or delegating any of your work, learning to become a leader is going to be a highly effective asset to your business which we will delve deep into in this book. The best leaders are the ones who know how to govern themselves, and learning to govern yourself is going to be one of the most crucial aspects of freelancing that we will cover in the coming chapters.

There will be a long road ahead before you can reap the rewards of financial stability through freelancing, which makes it important that people do not focus exclusively on the end goal but on learning to appreciate the process.

A Glimpse Into Freelancing

Before getting started with our freelancing education, we will explore the key points that will be addressed in this chapter so you can have an idea of what are the most important considerations that a person must have in mind when wanting to succeed as a freelancer.

A freelancer is someone who asserts themself as an expert in their field toward people who are looking to do business with people who are very knowledgeable in a specific niche area of business. The first few chapters will delve into how a freelancer can astutely go about figuring out what is the best niche industry they should do business in and who is the target audience for that niche. This book will explore how there are both internal and external factors that go into this decision.

Secondly, freelancers always have to contend with other freelancers who are doing business in the same niche, and therefore, trying to attract clients from the same target audience. These other freelancers are known as your competitors and you must be as knowledgeable about them as you are about your own business.

There are several different places where a freelancer can do business. Since freelancing has grown so considerably in popularity, there are several online places that can become a freelancer's office. Online platforms let freelancers handle all their responsibilities while still allowing them to be flexible with their time and location. Knowing which is the best platform for your situation is critical to ensuring you are wise with your time. Choosing the wrong platform for your situation can lead to a lot of missed opportunities and complications in the long run, which we will explore in more detail in chapter three.

Knowing how to interact and collaborate with clients is one of the most crucial things freelancers need to learn to do productively. The two things freelancers must always be working to achieve when interacting with clients is securing repeat business and acquiring new business. There is a lot to client interactions that can only be learned by going through those experiences, but there is also much knowledge that can be imparted to emerging freelancers to help them know what to avoid and what to look for when trying to get work.

Lastly, it is important to make a note of how important it is to ensure you always consider yourself a student of freelancing. Being an effective freelancer entails that you are always learning new things about your industry, your competitors, the business of freelancing, and yourself. Learning to have a success-oriented mindset is critical, too. Since no one is going to hold you accountable for your actions and decisions, you must learn to keep your mind focused on the things that allow you to be productive so that you do not feel overwhelmed by all the work that is required to succeed as a freelancer.

With all the moving parts required to be a professional freelancer, it can seem daunting to consider all the work it takes to master each responsibility and requirement in a balanced and focused way. Therefore, it is very helpful to read this guide into freelancing to learn the most effective strategies of how to efficiently address what will be required of you as you develop your skills and expertise.

Freelancing is not an easy journey but one that is open to anyone who wants to take their aspirations of professional autonomy and manifest them into reality. The most important consideration that can be communicated to anyone just getting started with freelancing is that they are not just starting a new job, but getting ready to embark on an endless journey. There is no finish line when it comes to freelancing, just ways to make the journey less bumpy and more smooth. Every day you wake up with the conviction to become the best freelancer you can, you are opening the door for opportunities you could never have imagined and that can only happen to you and no one else. Be resilient, patient, and passionate about what you do.

Let's get started.

Chapter 1: Finding Your Freelance Niche

Identify your niche and dominate it. And when I say dominate, I just mean work harder than anyone else could possibly work at it. –Nate Parker

You would not show up to a gym wearing hockey pads, cleats, and boxing gloves. While it may be possible for you to train for different sports in a single training session, you will find better success by defining what area of sports you want to participate in and leave your mark in.

Perhaps a better way to phrase this sentiment is by conjuring the now somewhat cliché expression, "the riches are in the niches." Although slightly overused, there is no denying that there is truth to that statement. Knowing what niche you are going to conduct business in is the equivalent of putting your glasses on and seeing things in a clearer and more focused way. Moreover, knowing your niche does not only provide better visibility for you but also for your prospective clients; it positions you in the spotlight of a specific room filled with people looking at the stage ready to be dazzled by a business proposition worth their while.

This chapter will shed light on the importance of defining what niche you are going to be tackling as a freelancer, and will also detail the best ways to go about discovering which niche is best suited to you. Furthermore, you will also learn how to segment and establish yourself as an authority of that specific niche to prospective clients by providing unique selling points that are specific to your offering and that go above and beyond what the competition has to offer.

There are freelancers who are venturing into this lifestyle more as a result of them already chasing a specific niche that they enjoy working within, and that are using freelancing as a method to monetize their pre-existing passion. For those of you who fall into this category, this chapter will help you with knowing how to market that passion in a way that is attractive to clients, learn to combine it with other niches and set yourself apart from the competition so you can always confidently and effectively pitch your offering to anyone at any time.

Perhaps a decade ago, when freelancing was not as popular as it is now, there wasn't such an imperative need to pick a niche since there was less competition. This is not the case anymore. The simple truth is that it is not enough to be a freelancer who offers quality services to others. You now have to find a way to distinguish yourself and make your business cater to the needs of those willing to pay for your services. Doing this entails that you examine and recognize the market you are entering so that you can build a sound strategy on how to penetrate it with a strategy that will deliver continual growth.

Deciding upon a niche allows you to assert yourself as an expert in your field, which in turn enables you to market yourself as such and consequently charge more for your services. You would not be able to do this if you were offering graphic design services from a business that also caters to those in need of content writers.

Clients are looking for people who are the best in their field, which is why they are outsourcing to other businesses in the first place and not delegating it to a department in their own company. People are willing to pay extra to ensure they are purchasing expert services, as opposed to just another service in an otherwise stacked freelance offering.

It may sometimes seem illogical to suggest that narrowing your options is beneficial for your work, but in this case, pursuing a smaller market segment will in the long run be more profitable than if you try and do business with every person you find along the way. This might not be the case initially when getting your business started, but in the long run, you will ensure that you become progressively better at your craft and also meet people from the same industry who can help you with your networking responsibilities, a crucial component of freelancing.

Defining your niche will enable you to concentrate your efforts in a more productive way. It is normal to feel unsure of what the right niche for you is or to feel motivated to try as many different niches as possible to find the one that would be most beneficial for you to work in.

Freelancer Viktor Marinov expounds on the importance of defining your niche in his latest article by stating the following: "Talk to people who focus on different things and think about what drives them. Does it sound like something that you could be into? Try it out. Think of it like this—you have five different kinds of candy. You can either keep eating without switching out of convenience or alternatively try all five and find out what you like most".

This quote by Marinov highlights the benefits of giving yourself the opportunity to experience different niches before making your mind up about which one will ultimately become the niche you focus on for the rest of your freelance career.

Swimming With the Current

If you are a nascent freelancer who is seeking to establish yourself as a confident and successful solopreneur, it is essential that you find the right niche. Discovering your niche is a very personal endeavor, since it will require you to be introspective about your skills, aspirations, and preferences. However, there is also a degree of pragmatism that you must employ when discovering your niche. There is no denying that you will be much more successful doing something you love for work, but it is also true that a person is likely to achieve a lot more by swimming with the current as opposed to against it; which is why knowing where the money is going in terms of freelance work is a critical consideration to have in mind.

There are some niches which inherently possess more earning potential than others. If your goal is to make as much income as possible out of freelancing—there is nothing wrong with this being your aspiration—then you should look at the many tools the internet provides for people trying to see where the money lies.

Some novice freelancers are already working a job they love, but conversely, their passion is not providing the sufficient income they need to maintain themselves and their dependents. For that reason, some people turn to freelance as purely a money-making scheme, so they are not forced to leave the work they love doing. For those people and countless others, I would suggest looking into industry trends and what businesses are doing to stay relevant and competitive in those markets. Being aware of what is being done in a specific niche is a great way to understand your competitors and find potential gaps in the market that you can fill with a new idea or strategy.

However, be wary of becoming too enticed by niches that are rapidly rising in popularity. Just because something is sought after right now does not mean that it will stay that way one year from now. Many aspiring freelancers jump to work in the niche that is receiving most attention at a given moment, unaware that they have to also consider the "evergreen niches." Evergreen niches refer to niches that, although it might not be the new and hottest thing in the business world, still maintain a steady level of attention and traction in the marketplace to make entering that niche a worthwhile and profitable endeavor.

An easy way to get started on your market research is to use Google Adwords. Google Adwords is a powerful tool in seeing how much businesses are willing to pay for keywords that are relevant to the market you are considering entering.

Let's say you did a search on Google Trends and found that graphic design has been receiving prolonged worldwide attention for the past ten years with high popularity. Google Trends ranks popularity from a scale of zero to 100 and also shows you related topics after each search, which you can pursue to potentially combine niches or find one that you believe has the potential to increase in popularity over the coming years.

Now that you want to discover as much as you can about how the graphic design market is doing, you can input graphic design into Google Adwords and examine the CPC (cost-per-click) rating of the advertisements related to that industry. Doing so enables you to determine how much businesses are willing to invest into advertising.

Here is a brief list of the current highest-paying freelance jobs out there in the market:

- IT
- cryptocurrency
- engineering
- accounting consultancy
- graphic design
- marketing

Looking Inward

However, as we all know, money isn't everything. It is true that you can make a substantial amount of money as a freelancer, but one of the added freedoms that comes with the territory is the opportunity to work in a field that you are genuinely passionate about. Moreover, freelancing allows individuals to exercise and flaunt their natural or practiced abilities in a way where they can get paid to utilize their strengths in a professional setting.

Regardless of what your goals are, finding a niche should be an endeavor where you strive to strike a productive balance between finding something that is monetarily profitable and also enjoyable.

Being a novice at freelancing should not inherently mean that you expect to be a novice at the niche you ultimately decide to pursue. There are, of course, individuals who take up freelancing in a market where they have no prior experience in working, and some of these individuals manage to thrive and make it work for them. Still, going about things this way is significantly more challenging than if you decide to pursue a niche where you are already experienced in.

Thinking about your hobbies, interests, skills, talents, and prior experience is a great place to start. Just because you are new at freelancing does not mean that you should conduct yourself as a beginner in the field you are about to enter. Suppose you have professional experience in a certain sector, or perhaps you have diligently been pursuing a specific hobby that you have become impressively adroit at doing. In that case, you can use this experience as a portfolio to show prospective clients and use it to assert yourself as an expert.

Here are three considerations to bear in mind when trying to decide what niche would be best suited for your interests, skills, and past experience:

1. *The Best or One of the Best*

Become either the best or one of the best at something. Providing great work to your clients can be a powerful form of marketing in the way of word-of-mouth and positive feedback. Regardless of how well you promote yourself, you will always need to have the talent to back it up. This is why it is critical that you not only work in a niche that promises a lot of revenue, but one that you can also become very talented in. In Scott Adam's article entitled "Career Advice" he professed that there were two options for any person looking to excel in a certain field:

> "...if you want something extraordinary, you have two paths: 1. Become the best at one specific thing. 2. Become very good (top 25%) at two or more things. The first strategy is difficult to the point of near impossibility. Few people will ever play in the NBA or make a platinum album. I don't recommend anyone even try. The second strategy is fairly easy. Everyone has at least a few areas in which they could be in the top 25% with some effort".

There is an important distinction to make between making yourself the best at something you have no experience or interest in and between continuing on the path of excellence you have been on for several years. If you have a passion which you have been pursuing for several years and have consequently developed heightened skills at that particular craft, there is no need or urgency to start looking for other disciplines so you can become very good at other things.

At the end of the day, when you are a freelancer offering services or products to business, it is not so much about what you can physically do for them as it is about what image you can portray to them, or how professional and reliable your brand appears to be in their minds. No one is going to audit whether you truly are the renowned expert you assert yourself to be. If you can deliver a project on time that meets the specific requirements of the client, and you have conducted yourself professionally and respectfully throughout the entire interaction, the deliverable that you send over will be proof that you are perfect for what that client is looking for, and you will have gained yourself repeat business.

If you believe that you can pursue a niche you feel is suited to your abilities and that will bring you the type of clients you would love to work with for the rest of your life, have no fear to assert yourself as the very best. A crucial component of working with clients is exerting confidence. If you are confident in what you are speaking about, clients are more likely to believe what you say. If you are hesitant or cannot answer their questions, they will doubt your authority and the validity of your credentials.

Even if what you deliver to them is not exactly what they envisioned, they will have no qualms or hesitation about reaching out to you and asking for you to address whatever issues they want you to fix. If they do not believe in your expertise, they are more likely to see the gaps in the project you delivered as a sign that you are not what they are looking for.

Therefore, do not feel like you cannot focus on just one niche because it will be virtually impossible for you to be the best in the world at one particular thing. If you do not want to expand your business offering into more niches but would love to continue becoming great at one specific thing, go forth and become excellent because the passion you exude will transfer into the work you do and the way you communicate to clients.

Of course, a big component of confidence is experience. You cannot pick up a new discipline one day and master it right, nor can you be confident in the skills you are only just beginning to forge. This is one of the reasons why you must be cautious as a beginner freelancer to not be too fastidious about the type of business you agree to manage.

2. *The Early Stages*

While it is important to find a niche and segment, the type of marketplace you want to do business in, the initial stages of freelancing, for example, the first two years should be all about getting your feet wet and learning as much as you can about the freelancing industry and yourself as a freelancer.

Even if you have decided to be a freelance graphic designer but get requests for content writing work, do not be so quick to say no. Even if you do not do the best work possible, you are learning how to interact with clients and also learning about which aspects of your day are best suited to your freelancing goals and which need adjusting for you to be more proactive.

Every freelancer dreams of working with their dream clients, and every freelancer has a different image in their mind of what that perfect client is. However, it is essential to consider if you are ready to do business with your dream client, because the only thing worse than not finding clients you enjoy working with, is finding them but having them leave you because your ways of doing business do not align.

Therefore, the first couple of years should be aimed at you conducting a trial and error of what works best for you in terms of schedule, routine, communication, workload, and of course, niche.

If you are someone who has abandoned their nine-to-five jobs to pursue freelancing, you might be inclined to continue the same schedule you followed when working as an employee. While this might work well for some, you might find that you are more proactive in the evening, or afternoon, and therefore need to create your own personalized schedule that allows you to always provide optimal performance output.

Furthermore, you might also discover that it is better for you to work Saturdays and Sundays, but take Mondays and Tuesdays off, as an example. One of the most enviable benefits of freelancing is that you can arrange your work around your personal life, instead of the other way around. Perhaps you live next to a school and prefer to work weekends when there is less noise, or you are attending an online course that requires you to study early in the morning, which leaves the evenings free for freelancing. The point is, do not become too bogged down or anxious about discovering who you are as a freelancer during the early stages because you are not supposed to know. Take the time you need to explore the freelancing sphere and do not be too hard on yourself when you make mistakes because these are the best times to make mistakes when you are not handling high-level multinational clients so you can afford to make the occasional error.

3. The 30-Day Experiment

Much of what you will learn during the first years of freelancing will be how to get clients. Knowing how to make others become interested in your brand is essential for success. Sometimes, regardless of all the data regarding popularity or demand and all the expertise or preconceived notions you may have about what niche you want to work in, the only way to discover what is the right niche for you is to see how well you can attract clients who belong to that specific niche.

With this in mind, I recommend you run a short experiment to see if you can attract clients in the first 30 days of attempting to do so while trying out a certain niche. You should not jump into the first niche that proves successful while undergoing the experiment, because you might be able to double or even triple the amount of clients you attract with a different one.

You should start by making a list of the top three most profitable niches and the top three niches you are most excited about pursuing; if some of these niches overlap, even better!

Once you do that, devise a strategy for how you will go about attracting clients to your brand (we will go into a more in-depth analysis of how to market yourself in chapter five). Be sure you have your plan of action written down because doing so will allow you to go back and revise what specific parts of your plan might need readjusting or perhaps to be expanded on because of how successful they were in your experiment.

Once you have your plan of action, give yourself a thirty-day timeline to try and get at least your first client. If after thirty days you have not been able to even capture the interest of a single prospective client, it might be time to reconsider that niche.

However, if you do get a client before the thirty days are up, don't stop the experiment and automatically call it a victory. Remember that you are also trying to compare your performance in one niche with several others. Just because you got one client in five days, does not mean that you will continue to get clients moving forward. Imagine you get your first client in your first five days, but then fail to get any more throughout the experiment. There is also the chance that while it takes you 15 days to get a client in a different niche, you might end up getting five times the amount of clients in the time that is left.

Therefore, complete the experiment by trying to get as many clients in thirty days as possible and see which niche performed the best for you.

Defining Your USP

Regardless of how perfectly your skills and your niche work with each other, you must find a way to set yourself apart from the competition. Unfortunately, being great at what you do is not enough these days to get the attention of prospective clients.

A critical component of your business strategy must be aimed at possessing an offering that is unique to you and that no other competitors are offering to their clients. Defining your unique selling proposition, or USP, can be quite challenging. The key to finding your

USP is to understand your clients, the competition, the market, and yourself.

To help you along this path, consider answering the following questions which will help guide you in defining your USP.

Who are you going to be helping by providing your services? Many times we become focused on what are the things we can do, but we lose sight of what others actually need as opposed to what they might become attracted to. Being able to help someone achieve something that must be done and that they cannot achieve themself is a great place to examine. Feel free to be proactive in your approach to seeking answers to these questions. You can ask people you know and perhaps even conduct a questionnaire to find out what the biggest pains businesses need addressing immediately. If there is a gap between what businesses want to be done in terms of their graphic design work that isn't being met by the people they have working for them, or by the freelancers or agencies they are working with, find a way that your skills can address those pain points.

What does your dream client look like? You do not have to be very descriptive with your answer to this question, because there is a lot you are going to learn about managing clients that you do not know yet. However, once you have built a robust portfolio that you can gladly brandish to big companies, it is important that you make sure you work with people who align with your vision and your work ethic. The goal of freelance work is to acquire repeat business, but if you are working with someone you do not want to ever work with again, you are wasting your time.

When answering this question, think about things like responsiveness, communication, and vision. Do you want to work with someone who is constantly communicating with you throughout the process or someone who leaves you to do your work and checks up every few weeks? Do you want to work with someone who communicates with you in a very professional and formal manner or someone who you can talk to in a relaxed and personal manner? This also depends on the specific niche you are working in.

Identifying what your ideal client looks like will inherently aid you in understanding the type of business you want to run as a freelancer. If you want to work with a client who is connecting you to other prospective clients, then you need to ensure that your marketing is on point and that you always leave enough time in your day to network with other people.

What two adjectives best describe your business? Some resources recommend finding three or four adjectives that are most suited to describe your business or the idea of the business you are in the process of creating. However, it is better to condense all your imaginative ideals into simply two words to really help you focus on what will make your business special, what sets it apart from the competition, and what components that you will focus on most while working on marketing.

For example, let's say that you envision your business to be creative, cooperative, innovative, and personal. These are all great attributes for any freelancer to have. However, the more adjectives you attribute to your business, the more space you are allowing for competitors to compete and match with what you are trying to provide to clients. Furthermore, it will be significantly harder to drive an underlying and clear message to people in your marketing initiatives if you are attempting to depict several different selling points.

For this reason, it is ok to start with three, four, or even five adjectives that best describe your business, but be prepared to scratch off as many as you need to until you are left with only two. In this scenario, we can imagine that we start off with the four aforementioned adjectives. By combining the understanding that we acquired about what specific skills and competencies set us apart from the competition, and what competitor freelancers are focusing on as their unique selling propositions, we learn what adjectives we need to keep and which need to go because they are already being used to market the business of other freelancers.

Think about it, the marketing you would see for a business that is cooperative and personal will look very different to one that is creative and innovative.

What do the products or services that you offer clients look like once they are finalized? Rather than sell what you can do for your client, offer what the finalized product will look like. People are much more interested in hearing about what they are going to get as opposed to hearing what a certain situation is going to entail.

Many freelancers try to market their services too simply by saying that they are going to write a great copy for their landing page. Even if the freelancing does in fact have the proven ability to do so, this type of language falls flat and does not give the prospective client a clear idea of what they will be getting once the collaboration has finalized.

Clients react more positively to aspirational and vivid imagery, rather than to incomplete ideals. Rather than ensuring to provide great written content, promise a 1,000 to 2,000 research based story that will increase both online traffic and sales by 5% by the first 10 days since writing the copy. In other words, be specific about how the business will profit from doing business with you.

Another important consideration to keep in mind when answering this question is ensuring that your service portfolio is not so expansive that it becomes counterproductive. Often, freelancers—especially new freelancers wanting to explode onto the scene—believe that the more the services they can provide and promote online, the more opportunities will come their way. However, while this might be true in the short-term, in the long run you will be facing many obstacles by not condensing your service offerings to a maximum of two different services.

The more services or products your business provides, the less likely you are to be perceived as an expert in any of them. This issue is not only true in terms of perception, but it is also a reality that a freelancer who has to dip his toes into several different fields will not be able to develop his skills at a productive rate.

By condensing your services to only two, you can ensure that every project you undertake will improve your skills and abilities within that chosen field. Moreover, it will be much easier for you to find your ideal client if you are already working in a niche that you enjoy.

Keep in mind that just because you only offer two different types of services that you cannot think big about what different iterations and manifestations those services can take. Imagine you choose to pursue writing as a freelancer. In that case, you offer content writing as one of your services, and under that service, you market your ability to provide content for academic articles, food blogs, ghostwriting, and SEO content creation for example. With writing as your only area of expertise, you can already cater to scientists, foodies, and high-level executives, which will all require very different work from you, but all will help you grow as a freelancer writer.

Start by choosing one or two services. Then, make a list under each one about the different types of business that service can provide for you and the different types of clients it can attract.

Do Not Preemptively Quit Your Job

Some people think that to fully commit to achieving success as a freelancer, you must quit your job and any lifelines to other careers to truly achieve the focus you need to succeed. However, it is best to ensure that you do not add unwarranted stress and urgency to your freelancing career, which will likely not immediately provide you with the financial security you need to quit your day job.

Freelancing requires that you manage many moving parts; having the added stress of not having the finances needed to sustain yourself during this time will cause you to not give the required attention and effort to the many tasks that will be on your table when starting out as a solopreneur. A general rule of thumb prescribed to freelancers is to ensure they have at least three to six months' worth of living expenses before quitting their job to solely focus on freelancing.

Learn How to Negotiate With Clients

Regardless of how sound and well-thought-out your contracts or business proposition may be, some clients are inherently more complicated than others and will want to adjust your proposals. As a newbie, negotiating can be challenging because you will feel inclined to accept whatever terms a client presents you with due to your eagerness to start working and to begin cutting your freelancing teeth. However, knowing how to negotiate terms with a client is an indispensable skill that all freelancers should have in their arsenal.

Although the best teacher will always be experienced, freelancing communities are a great place to reach out to more experienced freelancers to ask them about what they have learned about negotiating with clients.

Every client will be different, but some general strategies will help you along the way:

- Back up the reasons behind your prices with data that will support your terms when asked by a client.

- Do not rush into a contract. Some clients will want you to agree to their terms or provide some terms of your own right away. Rushing your negotiation can hinder your business, so do not be scared to tell your client that you need some time to iron out the specifics.

- See the negotiation as a collaborative effort that aims to make both parties happy. Do not venture into negotiating thinking with a mindset of not wanting to be fooled or duped by your client or thinking that you are going to outsmart them. Understand that negotiating a contract should consider the perspectives and needs of you and your client.

Master Your On-Boarding

First impressions count. Getting started with a client should be one of your top priorities as a freelancer, so leaving it to chance and spontaneity is not the best approach. Every freelancer should have a carefully constructed onboarding process where the client receives all the needed information that outlines what they can expect from the collaboration, how and when they can get in touch with you, deadlines, etc.

While it is imperative that you have this template ready so you do not have to create a new one every time you start a new project, do take the time to personalize it in the places that it needs to reflect the specifics of the client and the project you two are about to collaborate on. Clients will disengage if they feel they are receiving a cookie-cutter welcome reception, so modify where necessary.

Here are some steps to take to ensure you have a well-developed onboarding process:

1. Know your brand image so you can align it with your welcome message. If you market yourself as a youthful and dynamic freelancer, express that aspect of your business in your onboarding process.

2. Ensure that your contract reflects the local legislation to avoid fines and get lower tax rates.

3. Have the goals communicated by your client present in the onboarding process to show them that you have listened to the priorities they have expressed to you.

4. Provide detailed information regarding the times and the best way for the client to get in touch with you depending on the day.

5. Strike a productive balance between professional and personable.

6. Provide dates of when they can expect updates on the progress.
7. Make clear what you expect from them in order for you to be successful, such as transparency and professionalism.

Finding the right niche is one of the most fundamental and rewarding considerations every beginner freelancer must have when getting started on their journey toward gaining professional and financial autonomy.

Becoming aware of what your niche is going to be is the equivalent of being handed a map of the many places you are about to traverse. With this map, you can identify what you will need to equip yourself with to be successful on your journey and what obstacles you can expect to come across as you move forward.

Although this step does not entail any interactions with clients or any immediate incur financial gain, it is nevertheless the precursor to all the success you will achieve, so face it with a sound mind and a hungry heart. Equally important to finding your niche is identifying who are the people and businesses that move within that niche, for these will be the voices you will be in constant communication with as you grow in your chosen field.

Checklist

	Make sure that the industry or niche you are interested in becoming a part of is not showing any significant decline in its global performance to avoid swimming against the current of success.
	Exercise introspective research about yourself. Make a list of the professional experiences and skills that you enjoy exercising and you feel can be an asset to any professional entity looking to do business with a freelancer.
	Be patient and strategic at the beginning. While many people will praise the importance of being selective with the clients and work

	you accept, be aware of how the early stages of freelancing should be viewed as a learning experience where you learn important considerations about yourself as a freelancer and the way you interact with clients.
	Create a single sentence that describes what makes your business unique and special, and why businesses can benefit from implementing it into their strategies moving forward.

Chapter 2:

Identifying Your Target Market

If defining your freelancing niche is like being handed a map to your destination, understanding your target market is the equivalent of identifying the geography and the customs of each different town you are going to be visiting along the way.

Knowing what your target market looks like goes hand in hand with the understanding of what your niche is going to be; you cannot have one without the other. For this reason, the second chapter will be dedicated to explaining the best way to find out who your target market is going to be and how you can address their concerns and needs with your service offering.

Your freelancing services cannot benefit everyone, and nor should they. "The brands that speak to everyone speak to no one," says Morgan Brown, VP of Marketing for Shopify.

Your brand needs to constantly strike a productive balance between your unique selling points and the unique characteristics of the clients you are trying to attract and who are active participants in the industry you are doing business in.

Understanding your niche will help you in defining your unique selling points, and knowing your target market will help you understand the best way to communicate to them. By knowing the most effective way to market your brand, you can make your business proposition more attractive by adhering to the specific needs of the market and, ultimately, end up being able to command higher rates and increase sales.

Be sure to save your marketing initiatives till after you have understood your target market. Trying to create a message without any idea of who it is directed towards, or hoping that it will eventually fall into the right hands after throwing it to as many places as possible will make you lose valuable time and money. You will constantly be changing your promotion tactics to fit opposing markets that will never give you a consistent framework for you to work with. Therefore, the first step must always be research.

Research

Just because there are people looking for your services, it does not mean that they are all automatically prospective clients that you should be trying to do business with. There are many more considerations that every freelancer must bear in mind when trying to attract and communicate with clients other than looking for people in need of their freelancing services.

Doing target market research entails that you understand who the clients are paying money to get services related to your niche, and who are the freelancers they are doing business with. However, an important consideration to keep in mind is that the research you will do to discover your most profitable target market is not geared toward finding what businesses have the most money to pay freelancers like you.

Just like you cannot proclaim that your target market is men or artists, you cannot be so general in your approach as to say that you are looking for businesses that are paying the most money to freelancers working in your specific niche. What you are trying to determine is which people will react most positively and become more easily engaged with the ideals and purpose of your brand so that you can obtain and retain faithful clients. It is very plausible that your target market might be businesses that do not have as much capital as other companies, but they are still the ones that are more susceptible and likely to engage with your brand and want to integrate the services or products it provides into their business model.

If you simply aim to attract the businesses that are spending the most money on working with freelancers in your niche, then you are not fully addressing the requirements of target market research. Even if you were to simply focus on creating a message that speaks with businesses with the most money, you will end up not making as much money as you spend on marketing because you will not be able to retain as many clients and you will constantly be creating new promotions and marketing initiatives to reflect the needs of every different businesses you are trying to attract.

Market research empowers you with the knowledge that you can use to customize the way you go about acquiring a client base. Without a comprehensive understanding of what your market looks like, you end up wasting time trying to connect with people who are not going to help you progress and might detract time and energy away from other more suitable clients.

Going about doing this research can be as simple as looking at the work portfolio of your freelancing competitors and identifying what companies they are working with and what type of work they have produced for them.

When conducting research, do not simply look at the most successful or recognizable freelancers; examine those which you feel most resemble your business offering, even if it involves looking at a freelancer who is not as successful or popular as others. The idea here is not to copy their approach but to get a general idea of the work they are doing so you become knowledgeable on the matter and inspired to perhaps create something that you feel will address needs your competitors are not addressing themselves.

Make a list of the companies freelancers similar to you have worked with and then understand those companies themselves in terms of the industry they are in, their size, and how they market themselves online. Once you have done this, use your imagination to think of what your ideal target market would look like, similar to how you were asked to imagine your ideal client in the previous chapter.

The Ideal Target Market

There are two things you must bear in mind when envisioning the type of market you want to attract, demographic and psychographic.

Demographic refers to things such as age, gender, professional, and geographical location among others. Psychographics refers to the intangible and intrinsic components of a person, such as their aspirations, their personalities, and beliefs. It is essential to consider both of these so you can have a well-rounded and complete comprehension of the type of people you want to do business with.

Then, compare the research you did previously with the list of qualities you want your target market to possess. Although you will most likely not be able to compare the psychographic considerations to anything, you can still fuse your aspirations with the reality of what is out there to forge a more concrete and realistic understanding of what you should be aiming for when searching for prospective clients.

It is important to complete these steps because many new freelancers simply look at who is doing business with other freelancers and believe that to be enough to understand their target market. However, by going about it this way you are disregarding what makes you unique and special. Sometimes, the way you want to do business is more important than the type of business others can provide for you, so be sure to put your specific ideals and requirements into the equation.

Four Questions to Consider

CEO of her own marketing firm, aptly named SherryMTotten after herself, Sherry expounds on the following when it comes to defining your niche: "Define your target audience by thinking about who they are, what their big challenge is and how your solution will uniquely and directly answer that challenge".

While it is important that you are aware of the struggles and the needs of your client, this does not mean that you should base your entire business on the solutions you can think of to the problems of other business people. Remember that your skills and experiences are what make you unique, and those personal traits are the tools you should expand, develop, and leverage to be confident and deliver services or products that are truly special and cannot be duplicated.

Defining your niche should always be a consequence of what you have already decided to do, which is why the previous chapter delved into knowing how to discover what area of freelancing you would like to tackle.

Discovering the right niche for you will require you to strike a balance between defining what is the most logical and productive extension of your work in terms of clients and also what are your preferences when it comes to knowing what type of people you like to work with, regardless of what area of freelancing you are working within.

Here are four easy but important questions you should try to answer so that you can identify the right client for you:

What is the general demographic of the client you are trying to reach? Knowing the basics such as age, and gender is the first step in effectively segmenting your future clients. For example, if you are trying to communicate with young adults or teens still in university, the way you promote your brand and the way you highlight the benefits your services can provide will be very different if you are trying to reach senior executives.

Perhaps you have quit your corporate job to pursue freelancing, which typically means that you are accustomed to working with adults in a professional setting. However, be prepared to consider doing things completely differently from what you are accustomed to. If you are offering services that are more geared towards a younger demographic, then you will need to educate yourself on the best ways to engage that type of client because it might not be something you are used to. In other words, there are skills that will be transferable to freelancing and others that you must be prepared to learn from scratch.

However, demographics need to be expanded far beyond age, gender, and location. The more specific we can get with understanding our target market, the more effective the message we are relating to prospective clients about our brand is going to be.

An effective model that is widely used in the field of marketing to discover a brand's target market is called the *TAM SAM TM.*

The *TAM* refers to the "total addressable market" and it is the largest scope from which to view your market. *TAM* encapsulates every person who could at any point be interested and have the ability to invest in your brand. For example, if you are working as a freelance illustrator, your *TAM* would be every person in the world who needs illustration services. While this is a good start, the total population in this sample is far too large for you to be able to create a meaningful message to promote your brand.

SAM stands for "Serviceable Addressable Market." This layer of market segmentation takes into consideration the specifics of our brand into the equation. The *TAM* focused exclusively on the exterior, while the *SAM* distilled the research a little bit more to look at which clients would be willing to buy not just the services of the niche we are working in, but the specific type of work that we do within that niche. Continuing with the example of freelance illustrators, *SAM* takes into account the *type* of illustrations that you do. This step is crucial because it references your unique talents that ultimately make up your business' branding. If you are a freelance illustrator who typically illustrates for fantasy novels or other manuscripts, then the *SAM* model would take this into account and disregard any businesses looking for an illustrator that did not need fantasy illustrations.

TM refers to the target market. This is the final step you take when segmenting your market. When finding your *TM,* you take into account all the other necessary considerations that are unique to your situation such as the type of client you want to work with or what businesses are most likely to work with you given the medium you use to market and promote your brand.

What business-related issues are your potential clients constantly facing that can be remedied by working with you? Every company faces issues, regardless of how much manpower or capital they have. For many companies, some problems persist for such a long time that the people working in that company forget that those issues can be taken care of and simply integrate those issues into their daily lives. Other times, people might not even be aware that they are doing things unproductively until they are informed by a third party. The point is that there is always room for improvement in any business, and that room should be occupied by your freelancing initiatives.

Some aspiring freelancers begin their journey of autonomy with this step, which is a form of reverse engineering the process. If you are looking to be as profitable as possible, then it is perfectly acceptable to begin defining your freelancing area of expertise by researching the market and getting an understanding of what aspects of business most companies are struggling with so you can forge an informed approach to defining your freelancing niche. However, the issue with going about things this way is that you will most likely need to educate yourself a lot beforehand if you are not well-versed in how to actually solve the specific issues you find in your research, and also that there are probably many other competitors who have gone about approaching the process the very same way, which leaves very little room for uniqueness.

Instead, it is better to look at ways that your freelancing work can remedy the problems many companies are facing. For example, if you find that journalism firms always post articles and blogs by the same in-house writers week after week, month after month, readers might be getting tired of always reading the same voices, especially if the written pieces are about opinions. Therefore, you could offer to be a writer that goes out on the field and interviews people about their opinions on certain matters, which might not be something that the employees of the firm have time to do with all their other responsibilities to the company.

If you cannot find a problem, then find a way to pose your services as an improvement on things that are working well but can be made to be even better. Say you are a freelance graphic designer; in that case, you could study the website of a prospective client and pitch to them ways that you could make it better. This approach is effective because if the company is not looking for someone to amend their struggles, then it means that there is less competition for you; however, the downside is that not every company is willing to have the way they do business challenged by an outsider, so every approach has its advantages and disadvantages.

What is the best place to reach your client?

Equally as important as knowing who your niche is going to be is knowing where they go to communicate with other businesses; in other words, what medium they use to promote themselves and seek others promoting their own businesses.

It is no use having the most effective strategy for a client who is going to deliver the most profits if you are unaware of what is the best way to reach them. Depending on the type of company you are attempting to do business with, you might need to focus your brand promotion exclusively on social media efforts, or in-person networking events among many other options.

There are companies that prefer to do business only with those who they have received personal recommendations about, and will not work with people that cannot be vouched for by others.

The idea is not to focus your entire business strategy on the preferences of other companies because you will hopefully be working with many clients who will most likely all have different ways of doing business. This consideration is why your promotion and marketing strategy should be malleable and adaptable to the needs of the different clients you work with.

How are your services the best option for businesses seeking to work with freelancers? It is not enough to simply offer a solution to a problem. As a freelancer, you need to ensure that your solution is promoted as the best solution to any business problem and that it cannot be rivaled by any competitor.

Sometimes the "problem" that you are trying to solve with your services doesn't even relate to any issue the client is facing, but in this case, the problem refers to an area of their business that can be improved by doing business with you. In this case, you will need to state how your services can benefit the client you are reaching out to by doing it in a way that presents the things that make you and your brand unique as an indispensable tool for that specific company.

Clients and businesses that you are seeking to attract like to feel like the message they receive from you is tailor-made and specifically formulated for them. Businesses that are seeking to outsource to freelancers or other third-party related providers are used to being pitched to constantly and therefore are adept at noticing when they are being sold a cookie-cutter promotion that reflects no real understanding or appreciation of who they are.

Ensure that your message, meaning the way you pitch your brand, aligns with the target market so that you do not waste your own time and the time of the potential clients. The best way to do this is to use the market research. You have to create a customized message that takes into account the things your prospective clients would like to hear about your brand and that you understand their values and priorities.

Aligning your message with your audience is critical, which is why it is essential to understand the specifics of your target market. If you adhere to the notion that your brand needs to cater to as many people as possible, without trying to segment yourself into a specific market, then you will either be forced to send out cookie-cutter messages that will interest no one, or you will end up personalizing every single pitch you make to cater to very different markets, wasting valuable time and resources in the process.

This final question requires that you understand what makes your brand unique first before moving forward. Knowing your strengths when compared to your competitors will allow you to present these to your prospective clients and use them as valid selling points to market your business.

The best way to identify your target market is to combine a detailed understanding of what makes you and your brand unique, with what makes the different clients who are able and likely to purchase your services similar. You should not be looking to find similarities in your prospective clients as a means to identify them in the first place, but as a technique to help your marketing efforts once you have already segmented them through research.

Obtaining a concrete understanding of your target market is more than just a competitive advantage, it is a fundamental requirement if you want to succeed as a freelancer. The more detailed you can get with the observations regarding who your target market should be, the more clients you will obtain and retain, which should be the ultimate goal of any freelancer regardless of their niche.

As it has been demonstrated in this chapter, segmenting the market into groups that you can deem viable clients requires thorough research and deliberation. However, there are ways to streamline this process and put yourself in the advantageous position of being part of a community that is constantly being put in contact with willing clients who are looking for freelancers just like you. If you are wondering how to go about getting yourself into these communities, then proceed on to the next chapter where we will explore how new freelancers have the option of both improving their professional skills while getting paying clients in the process.

Checklist

	Research the market that you are trying to enter with your freelance niche. Understand their demographic and what they are specifically looking for in a freelancer when deciding who to give their business to.
	Looking at the population sample of the market you are able to do business with as a freelancer, make a list of the type of clients you see reflected in your research and also make a list of your ideal client who you would like to work with, in terms of how you would like them to engage with you throughout a professional collaboration. Once you have both lists, compare the two and see.
	After you have identified your target market, create an overall idea of what these potential clients are looking for in a freelancer so you know how to position and promote your brand. Keep in mind the needs of the clients, but also what makes you special so that you can outshine the competition with skills and knowledge that only you can deliver.

Chapter 3:

Navigating Freelance Platforms

This chapter will look at how freelancers can leverage the rise in popularity of their industry to use the many online resources out there for freelancers to create their own virtual offices. With so many new choices of where to set up your online presence, it is imperative that you have a firm understanding of what each option offers freelancers so that you ensconce yourself somewhere that will be conducive to meeting and managing clients and to your overall success.

Being a beginner freelancer is, at best, a daunting situation. Unlike when you are an employee, you do not receive any paid training by a more senior colleague or a guidelines manual that you can peruse at your leisure to find out how to be successful at the company you are now a part of.

When you enter a new company, you can at least still count on the years of experience that the other people working there have had, which leads to an extensive portfolio of clients and projects that have built up a reputation that you can use to propel yourself forward into your new position. Suffice to say, this is not the case with freelancing.

The last chapter detailed the importance of defining your target market and how to go about doing that. While this is a crucial step that every novice freelancer must go through if they want to accelerate their success and invest their time and effort wisely, it is an entirely different consideration finding out the best way to get that target market to reciprocate the interest you surely have in doing business with them.

Chapter One elaborated on how to look inward into our unique skills and experiences so we can create an effective sales pitch for our brand. However, there are also resources that can help you do this while connecting you not only to clients but also to other freelancers who are just starting on their journey and might be feeling as lost as you are at times.

Remember how we mentioned that the early stages of freelancing should be viewed more as a learning experience? That is true, however, this does not mean that you should automatically expect to not be profitable during these initial stages.

Freelance platforms are websites geared toward connecting freelancers with potential clients. With the rise in the popularity of freelancing, many new platforms have been created and those that already existed have become the meeting space for thousands of creative individuals worldwide who have ensconced themselves in these platforms which have become like their office and their networking events all in one. Freelance platforms help give freelancers a platform to present their brands, construct a portfolio of work that they can brandish when pitching for new work, and get in touch with both clients and other freelancers from anywhere across the globe.

There is more than one type of freelance platform available and we will discuss them both; however, whichever one you decide to pursue, it is imperative that you take your business online and use a platform to do businesses as a freelancer. The age we live in now will not allow someone to be profitable unless they can exhibit their work online and get in touch with people through this medium.

Therefore, regardless of what site you use, be sure to peruse all the options available to you because just like understanding the right market to penetrate is crucial to your success, so is defining what platform is going to be best for you.

Freelancing Platforms vs. Job Boards

The two best options every freelancer has at their disposal when searching for a site to do their work are freelancing platforms and job boards.

Both of these options give you the opportunity to communicate with potential clients who are looking for freelancers and do business with and they both have their advantages and disadvantages. However, when it comes to those who are only just getting started on their freelancing journey, one of these options is highly more advisable than the other.

Whether you are on a platform or perusing a job board, both these sites act as the bridge between the profiles freelancers create on the sites and the clients who can also create profiles and post the projects they need to be finalized. Communication can happen both ways, either a freelancer finds a project they want to work on and get in touch with the client to request to work on that project, or the client picks a freelancer they feel would be right for their project without posting anything about the work that needs to be done on the site.

You can imagine these sites to be marketplaces where what you are looking for is sometimes also looking for you.

Freelance Platforms

Freelance platforms offer a more inclusive experience that goes beyond simply connecting freelancers with clients. These sites are designed to be the hub for aspiring freelancers who want to concentrate all their interactions, networking, communication, and project-seeking tasks at the same place. Freelance platforms are designed to become the virtual office of freelancers, which can be very helpful, especially to those who are just starting their freelancing journey and do not yet have an expansive portfolio that they can show clients.

Brand vs. Person

The advantage of using a freelance platform is that most of these sites take care of many aspects of freelancing for you, such as knowing how to market yourself to prospective clients. However, in terms of using these platforms, you would not be so much marketing your brand but yourself as a freelancing individual. Since brands are designed to promote businesses, these types of platforms are not the medium for this type of promotion. The only business that clients using this online service are supposed to be aware of is the one facilitating the platform they are on.

Although this might sound discouraging to those solopreneurs who wish to create businesses around their skills, it is crucial to remember the importance of being able to sell one's abilities and experiences before thinking about creating a brand around it. Many industry professionals stress the importance of regarding yourself as a salesperson before you ever consider yourself a freelancer. Building from this logic, you need to be able to have a firm grasp about what are your strengths and weaknesses before you can begin to turn your freelancing efforts into a business. For this reason, using a freelance platform is the best alternative for people who are only just getting started with freelancing and could use all the guidance they can get.

Streamlined Interactions

While it may feel slightly constrictive for some people to have all their interactions with clients and fellow freelancers confined to occur solely on the platform, this allows for easier supervision, guidance, and accountability in terms of fairness between freelancer and client.

Sometimes, even the client who falls directly into our target niche and who checks all the boxes of the type of people we would aspire to work with can behave themselves immorally and leave freelancers feeling dejected. For whatever reason, they might refuse to pay or fail to regard the work that has been done in a reasonable amount of time, making the freelancer wonder if all the work they did was in vain. There are many things that can go wrong when it comes to freelancer and client interactions, which is why having all the interactions confined to the same platform is more of an asset than it is a hindrance.

If a client fails to inspect the work that has been done, most of these platforms have deadlines and guidelines in place that ensure freelancers get remunerated for their efforts regardless of how unresponsive or uncooperative a client may be. Furthermore, there is always a mediator that works for the platform that can oversee the communication between the client and freelancer. This helps to protect the freelancer but also ensures that freelancers can receive the proper guidance in case their interactions are not as professional as they should be.

Support

The support that beginner freelancers need during their first endeavor into freelancing goes beyond just knowing how to effectively communicate with clients. Many of these platforms offer tutorials and other guidance resources that teach freelancers how to market themselves and make their profiles as attractive as possible to prospective clients.

Without these platforms, freelancers are left to do their own research and conjure ideas on the best ways to promote themselves that might not be as effective as they think. Not only are freelance platforms run by people who are experts in their field, but these sites also allow freelancers to connect with other freelancers who might have more experience and can guide those who are just getting started. Sometimes, just being able to get moral support is enough when it comes to this type of work. As popular as freelancing is becoming in modern society, it is still unlikely that you will be exposed to other freelancers in normal life since that type of work normally entails that you work from home. If you complain about the trials and tribulations of someone who works a nine-to-five job for a big company, they are most likely not able to relate or understand the challenges you are facing in your line of work.

Having the platform to rely on allows you to converse with other freelancers about the challenges they are facing and also receive advice on how to productively move forward. Freelancing can be a lonely endeavor, so having that support system goes a long way, even if you are an established freelancer with years of experience.

Portfolio

When you are starting out, you will not have a body of work to vouch for the assertions you are making to prospective clients about your work ethic and the project you can deliver to them in a timely fashion. This consideration can make it very challenging for new freelancers to find work since clients are always interested in finding the best freelancer they can for their projects.

The good news is that freelance platforms have a way of remedying this issue. Freelance platforms help position you as an expert regardless of your previous experience or lack thereof. They do this by shifting the focus on promoting yourself and your skills in a way that is concise and appealing to the person perusing your profile.

If you are a freelance writer, the platform might ask you to write a sample for them so they can gauge your skill level. If you write them a very good sample, you could very well be positioned at the highest tier of the company, without ever having conducted a single project. This way of helping freelancers, matched with the right guidance on how to promote yourself, can lead clients to see you as an authority in your chosen field.

Job Boards

Payment Fee

As useful and beneficial as freelance platforms are, they do have a downside when it comes to compensation that is not the same as job boards. Since there is so much support given to freelancers by these platforms, they inevitably take a commission fee from what the client pays you for your services.

It is natural that this is the case since at the end of the day, these platforms are a business that needs to be profitable for them to continue helping freelancers on their journeys. This is not the case with job boards and it is one of the advantages that opting for this service would be better than going with a freelance platform.

When a freelancer finds a project or a client they would like to engage with professionally, they get in touch and are able to negotiate prices depending on the experience of the freelancer.

While this may sound like it is awarding more freedom to the freelancer, which it is in a way, it is also providing more work and more opportunity for an inexperienced freelancer to communicate inefficiently, which can be quite detrimental when it comes to price negotiations.

Furthermore, when you are a beginner freelancer, your lack of a body of work will make it very challenging for you to have much negotiating power once you do find a client who wants to pay for your services, which is a challenge within itself. However, if you are already established and experienced, the situation is different and you can award yourself the freedoms that you are more likely to find on job boards as opposed to freelance platforms, namely, not having to split your payment to a freelance platform as a form of commission every time you finalize a project.

Communication

Some freelance platforms require that freelancers create a new alias for their platform, which is done mainly to protect the anonymity of the freelancer. Moreover, all communication is fully centralized within the platform and most platforms enforce strict policies that prohibit clients from communicating with freelancers anywhere outside their platforms and vice versa.

When it comes to job boards, the only way to get in touch with potential clients is to do it directly yourself. While some freelancers independently manage ways of protecting their real names, job boards do very little to facilitate what some freelancers consider to be very important for their business.

Since there is no chat room or messaging service with job boards, freelancers have no alternative other than to connect with them by their own means. While it is perfectly plausible to focus all your correspondence with your client entirely through email, this can get quite tiresome after a while and either the freelancer or the client will want to have a more direct and instant way of getting in touch with you, especially if the project is very demanding and intricate.

While this may be off putting to some freelancers, there are those who often relish in the ability to have more mobility in terms of communication and not be confined to a platform. This is a consideration that depends both on the personality of the freelancer and also on the niche.

If you are a freelance writer who spends most of their time sitting behind their computer typing away for hours, it will probably not be too outlandish to accept communicating exclusively via a specialized platform since your work does not require you to be mobile or away from your computer.

However, if you are a freelance videographer, working on creating audiovisual content which requires you to constantly be displacing yourself from several different locations to get the shots you need, it can be quite arduous to have effective communication with the client by having to sit and connect to the platform each time.

The same is true for PR or branding professional freelancers. This type of work might not be as itinerant as the one of a videographer, but it will require you to be constantly updating your client on the performance of the campaigns they assign you to work on.

So, Which Is Better?

As has been shown in this chapter, there is no conclusive answer as to which option is better between opting to work within a freelancing platform or perusing the job boards to independently manage your projects.

That being said, if you are not yet established as a freelancer in your field and are in the early stages of this professional endeavor, using a freelance platform will be more beneficial to you than getting started straight with the job boards.

Freelance platforms can be powerful launching pads for aspiring freelancers who might be feeling overwhelmed or confused about how to get started with managing all the different moving parts of the business they are trying to single handedly construct.

If used wisely, these sites can be the training ground for you to learn many valuable lessons about how to market yourself, communicating with other freelancers and prospective clients, identifying the right project from the wrong project for you, working alongside collaborators such as editors in the case of freelance writers and many more things.

The best thing about these platforms is that you are free to make mistakes in a controlled environment. There are times when the administrators who run these platforms gladly step in and do all promotions for you when they get contacted by clients who are looking for the right person to handle their business. Perhaps you are an aspiring graphic designer who has no experience in the industry but has signed up to work on one of these platforms as a freelancer but cannot generate any interest from prospective clients. If the site is credible, the admin will often recommend you and any others who are struggling to get work and vouch for your abilities to see the project through.

Once you are more experienced and feel that you have enough work under your belt to be able to manage your own business, job boards are a great place to connect with people and find work. This is especially important if you are attempting to transition into creating your own brand separate from any other freelance entity since there are occasions when the work you do on freelance platforms belongs to the owners of the platform and cannot be used as marketing material for your brand.

Too Much too Soon

A crucial consideration to put forth to any aspiring freelancer wanting to get as much work as possible, which is the case with many novice freelancers, is to be wary of signing up to too many platforms at the same time.

If you want to succeed as a freelancer you will inevitably have to exercise patience. As you begin to develop your skills and your portfolio, there will be an extended period during the beginning of your efforts to find any interested clients. The best advice that you can get is to be patient and seek the advice of those who are in the same niche and have been doing it longer than you have.

One thing you want to stay away from is signing up to as many platforms as you can under the notion that the more places you are active as a freelancer, the more opportunities will come your way. The truth is that this is a misguided practice.

Freelance platforms do everything they can to support your professional growth while connecting clients to the right freelancer. One of the ways they do this is by implementing an algorithm that determines which freelancers are performing the best, in terms of work volume and quality, and suggests those overperformers first to any client who goes online looking for someone to manage their projects. If you are spreading yourself too thin by trying to be active on several different platforms, you will be unable to be outstanding in any of them because you will be juggling several different projects all with varying guidelines on how they have to be managed.

You will also struggle to remember what are the specifications of each platform, which can lead to confusion and mistakes being made. The best outcome that can come about signing up to more than two platforms is that you will achieve moderate but not outstanding success at some of the platforms you are a part of, but will not be considered one of the better freelancers because you will not be able to keep up with the workload.

As frustrating as it can be at times, the lack of work at the beginning is actually a benefit that should be leveraged. Rather than dive headfirst into two orders immediately when you start out, it is better that you take the time you are given to work on your promotion and branding. Moreover, if you focus exclusively on just one project during your early stages as a freelancer, you will have more ability to focus on the specific requirements and ensure that you do good work that will help build both your portfolio and your confidence.

Finding the Right Platform

Freelance platforms are key for getting started on your freelancing journey for the various reasons we have already explored. However, this does not mean that you should join any platform without knowing what to look out for because not all of them will be as conducive to your success as others.

Pricing Model

One of the most important things you should be looking for in a platform is the ability to be motivated to continuously develop your skills and be compensated for that professional development. The best way for this to happen is to be part of a freelance site that offers different pricing models based on your level of expertise. Along with it being a fair way to differentiate between the different skill levels that are going to be present in the platform, it also serves as an incentive to acquire more experience and work harder to reach the higher tiers that pay more money and that are more attractive to prospective clients.

Some platforms offer a general pricing model that offers a fixed price for every freelancer regardless of their skill level or the difficulty of the project they are taking on. This model creates a ceiling that does not motivate you to work harder or become more adept at your skills. Be sure to avoid these types of platforms and always opt for the ones that value and acknowledge your professional development.

Another consideration entails that you compare the different fees each platform takes as commissions from the projects you take on. While it is normal that the company retains some of your income, you should strive to avoid those that retain more than 20% which is the industry average.

Target Platform

Lastly, think about what are the things you find most important about joining one of these platforms. There are freelancers who value the communal aspect of working on these sites more than anything else and therefore would prioritize being able to connect and communicate with others on the platform more than anything else.

There are other freelancers who might find that they want as much independence throughout their work as possible, so would prefer to work with a platform that gives freelancers as much freedom to complete their projects as possible.

Figure out what are the things you value most about being a freelancer and ensure that the platform you are looking into joining reflects those values in the way it connects you to clients and nurtures your professional development.

Regardless of what specific niche you are in, there are websites that cater to all the different freelancing disciplines by providing the advantages to freelancers that we have already expanded on. Although they are all focused around connecting freelancers with clients, there are differences among these sites which make some more desirable to work with.

Upwork

If you are a freelancer looking at finding the most recognizable and used platform out there, you have probably heard of Upwork, and if not you most certainly will.

Upwork is considered the largest freelancing platform in the world, and with over three million projects posted every year, it is easy to understand why. So much traffic means that there are more prospective clients posting their projects on Upwork than on any other site, but it also means that there will be more competition between freelancers.

Some of the reasons why Upwork is so popular is because of how flexible it is in terms of the contracts it offers freelancers. Freelancers have the choice of working with both short and long-term contracts or simply charging an hourly rate. These options are available to all freelancers regardless of how experienced they are. Furthermore, these contracts protect freelancers from being solicited for free work, sometimes disguised as requests for work samples, which is strictly prohibited on Upwork.

Fiverr

Fiverr is also a name you might have heard of due to their increased spending in marketing, especially in social media. Fiverr is an alternative to Upwork and although it does not manage as many freelancers on Upwork it is still a very worthy option.

One of the common criticisms regarding Fiverr revolves around how it compensates the freelancers using the platform. The commission fee that Fiverr takes from the money clients pay freelancers is higher than the industry average and payout can take from one to two weeks. Considering that freelancers need all the money they can get when getting started on this venture, having to wait two weeks to get paid can be very demoralizing.

LinkedIn

While the previous platforms are more niche and specifically geared to address the specific requirements of freelancers, LinkedIn is one of the most popular social networking sites and definitely the most popular employment-focused platform for professional people looking to connect and find work.

LinkedIn is unlike the previous two examples in that it is not designed for freelancers, but if used correctly, can be the best tool for any freelancer wanting to give their profile exposure and get in touch with prospective clients.

LinkedIn allows you to create attractive and informative profiles, peruse and interact with prospective clients, showcase your skills, and engage with other freelancers all for free. There is the option of paying for LinkedIn Premium, which will deliver a few more advantages, but most of what you already get for free with LinkedIn you would have to pay for in other sites that are geared specifically for doing business with freelancers.

Furthermore, LinkedIn gives you more space to showcase yourself and to provide links and detailed insights into your accomplishments and your personality than any other paid site. Other sites force you to condense and dilute your efforts to sell yourself and your business to prospective clients to fit the framework of their platform, but LinkedIn offers a wide variety of ways to do one of the most important things any freelancer can do during their workday…sell.

Before regarding yourself as a freelancer, you must learn how to be an effective salesperson in order to create credibility for what you are offering. Without credibility, no matter what you show a client, they will not be interested in doing business with you because they do not believe what you are selling is genuine or as valuable as you proclaim it to be.

By using LinkedIn, you can see what businesses are looking for in the professionals they are wanting to engage with by viewing the keywords that they use when specifying and detailing the requirements for a specific job. If you are a freelancing graphic designer, you don't have to pay to peruse job postings relating to that field and see what competencies and experiences recruits are looking for. By knowing these keywords, you can implement them into your profile—such as the LinkedIn header feature—to ensure that your profile is tailor-made for the type of client you want to do business with.

A great example of how a freelancing writer can use LinkedIn to grow professionally is to use the site as their writing platform and create a daily content schedule. LinkedIn encourages people to write blog posts or simply share their professional insights on their profiles to boost engagement on the site. Rather than having to adhere to someone else's schedule or specifications, you can write daily blog posts about any subject you want and post them on LinkedIn and use the platform as your own portfolio that is constantly being showcased to potential clients who can be directed to your content by how much engagement you can get.

Therefore, LinkedIn is the best solution to your quest to find the best platform to find freelancing work.

Having the right platform for your work is the equivalent of ensuring you have the right stage to perform your act. So far, we have looked into deciding what is the right performance we want to present, who is the audience we want to be attracting to our shows, and finally how to decide which is the best stage for what we are trying to present to the world—to keep the metaphor going.

All of these things must be considered and work harmoniously with each other if they all serve as the stepping stones towards the success we are guaranteed to have if we address all the vital considerations of becoming a top freelancer.

The next thing we must learn how to do correctly is learning the proper way to address the crowd who is watching and expecting us to dazzle them with our performance. Even the best action, with the best crowd and the best stage, will fail if we cannot understand how to engage our paying clients.

Checklist

	Understand the crucial differences between freelance platforms which are better for new freelancers, and job boards, which are better for more experienced freelancers.
	Freelance platforms offer a variety of support systems for beginners that can help develop their skills in a safe and productive environment. Take your time selecting the right platform and identifying if they offer you things you could not achieve yourself by running your own website.

	Job boards provide a lot more autonomy for freelancers, but they are better used when the freelancer has already acquired sufficient experience to present an impressive and substantial work portfolio. Once you feel you have produced enough work to create a robust portfolio, consider graduating to job boards, which will give you more creative freedom.
	Allow yourself to start slowly when you begin seeking clients. Do not give in to the misguided desire to acquire as many projects as possible, but instead allow yourself to focus on one project at a time and learn how to go about doing so properly.
	Do not just sign up to any platform you find; instead, look into their pricing model and ensure that the priorities you have as a freelancer are reflected in the way they do business and the way they manage their freelancers.

Chapter 4:

Managing Client Relationships

Knowing how to manage client interactions is one of the most fundamental skills every freelancer must acquire if they are to be successful in their chosen field. Just like every freelancer is different, every client will be different too. The best way to learn is by going through the process and acquiring enough experience so that you know how to engage with people in a way that makes them trust you with their business and has them coming back for more once a specific project has been completed.

Since you will be the head and voice of every department of your business, it is imperative that you deliver the best client service you can because even more important than the quality of the finalized product you deliver is the quality of the service you provide for the client.

The way you engage and communicate with a client has to not only be professional, but it must also align with the values and competencies that are represented in your brand, even if your brand is simply yourself and you do not have a business yet. If you can secure the trust of your client, they are much more likely to believe what you have to say throughout a particular collaboration and will be more forgiving if you ever need to ask for an extension or if you make a mistake along the way.

As crucial as it is to know how to conduct client relationships, it is also one of the hardest aspects of the job. As it has already been established, freelancing requires a lot of work to be done by yourself and requires that you summon a lot of confidence, perseverance, and resilience in yourself when trying to make opportunities happen for yourself and by yourself. The moment you begin engaging with a client can be stressful, especially if you are just starting out because it is the first real test of what you have been building so far and it can also be the first stepping stone into manifesting your freelancing efforts. However, a client is not aware or necessarily concerned with what it has taken for you to get to the place where you can have a conversation and pitch your business to them, which can make the way they speak to you seem dismissive and condescending. In these moments, it is crucial to remember to not take anything personally and that your best course of action is to remove the emotional component out of the equation. A client is there simply to acquire the business and find the person who they consider is best suited to work alongside them in bringing their vision to life.

Unlike when you are an employee of a larger company, your bad client service does not reflect badly on the company but on you personally, and getting a bad reputation is something that you cannot afford to do in the freelancing gig.

Building a robust and positive reputation is paramount to being successful as a freelancer. Half of your success will come from repeat business. If you can get a client to assign to your future upcoming projects and to speak of you positively through word of mouth to other businesses looking to do work with freelancers, you are securing future earnings that you can invest back in the business. Moreover, dealing with a client who you already have experience working with creates a much more comfortable and easy-going collaboration that will require less work than when you are conversing with a new client. Moreover, once you have already worked with a client once, you already know the specifics of how they like to do business and communicate, so you can be more efficient in the way you engage with them and in the way you structure your projects to meet their preferences.

It is true that it is important to focus on working with clients that you feel you can have a productive working relationship with, but during the early stages of your freelancing journey, it is best to get as much experience and context of what is out there as you can and to also begin building a name and a reputation in your niche industry.

The following chapter will provide detailed and comprehensive resources on the best way to go about communicating and collaborating with clients so you can reel them into giving you their business and also ensuring that they continue working with you on all their future projects.

Three Reasons Why Client Relationships Are Important

Ensuring positive and productive relationships with your clients can only garner positive results, even if it entails doing your best to leave your collaboration on a good note after dealing with a bad client.

With the rise in e-commerce and the benefits of customer retention, there are several reasons why being a professional collaborator is more important now than it ever was for freelancers.

E-Commerce

According to eMarketer, "US ecommerce sales will reach $794.50 billion this year, up 32.4% year-over-year". The pandemic is partly to blame for people's increasing interest and now reliance on online purchasing, which has made them less likely to physically go shopping at bricks and mortar stores. The same principle applies to businesses scouting for agencies or freelancers.

The rise in online presence is a tool that freelancers should take advantage of when devising ways to increase their brand exposure. The internet is the new shopping space for business people looking for entities that can take their projects onboard. Freelancers can build a positive reputation that helps cement their online presence by ensuring that every collaboration leads to positive word of mouth and recommendations.

Less Client Attrition

Statistics show that most businesses lose between 20-80% of their clients or customers every year because of ineffective client relationships. Losing clients can severely hinder the growth of your brand because it will put you in the position of constantly trying to play catch up and trying to undo the damage that was created by losing business.

The best way to grow as a business is to retain clients, and the best way to retain clients is to give them a positive experience when collaborating with them. One of the most effective ways to view how you should interact with your clients is to foster a long-term as opposed to short-term relationship strategy.

Some freelancers will pour all their energy and devote all their efforts into promoting their services to a prospective client with the ultimate aim of getting their business and securing a fresh paycheck. This way of doing business is not sustainable and is a representation of a short-term way of thinking.

A better way to look at the situation is to invest your energy equally into getting new clients, but also ensuring your efforts to provide a positive collaboration experience do not end the moment the project has been completed. Dedicate your energy into following up on all your clients and asking them how they are doing. Ask them if there is anything else you can help them with and update them on any changes in your business that you feel may apply to them and interest them.

"Word of Mouth" Marketing

Dragilev says the following in his article about the importance of client relationships, "...according to experts, a dissatisfied customer could tell around 13 people about a terrible service he got from your business. Therefore, you must take great care to monitor customer satisfaction to avoid having a bad reputation on the streets."

Generating positive word of mouth can do wonders for your business in terms of generating free marketing. However, a dissatisfied client can do a lot of damage by way of speaking negatively about their experience working with you.

It would be very unfortunate to have all your marketing and brand promotion initiatives hindered by a dissatisfied client. Even if the collaboration was lacking and the project did not turn out the way either of you envisioned it to, enact a long-term approach and follow up with your client. For example, if your client expresses to you their dissatisfaction with their collaboration with you, following up with empathy and understanding can do a great deal of damage control and prevent negative word-of-mouth marketing.

Becoming a Client Project Manager

When working as a freelancer, you effectively take on the role of client project manager that is normally assigned to a department, a group of people, or someone whose only job within a company is to be the constant liaison between someone working on a project for a client and the actual client.

As we have already established, a freelancer takes on every role within a company when taking on a new project. A freelancer will not only be responsible for getting the work done on time and to the client's specifications, but they also have to be the first and last line of defense when communicating the progress that is being made and any possible setbacks that might occur along the way.

In a way, this provides a necessary and beneficial sense of accountability that other project managers who sometimes end up taking the brunt of an upset client's outrage over the failings of someone else do not get to experience. Whatever you have to communicate to your client about the project will always be regarding something that is under your control and that you do not have to relay to a third party.

Providing a masterful piece of work to a client and being an effective liaison between your work and the client are two completely separate disciplines, and they both must be carefully executed if you are to build constructive professional relationships which is something you should always be striving to do as a freelancer.

Moreover, being pleasant and professional is not enough to provide the kind of service that you need to become effective as a client project manager. Everyone will have their strengths and will need to devote more time and energy into certain aspects of this discipline, but having a robust understanding of what are the most valuable and effective strategies to have when engaging a client is paramount to securing repeat business.

9 Tips on Ensuring Effective Client Relationships

The following strategies, or "tips," will ensure that the interactions you have with clients become more than just mere interactions but transcend to the point where they become relationships. The key word here is "relationship" because even though you are conducting business with a client, it does not mean that the human element should be removed from the interactions. Furthermore, you want to ensure that every relationship you have with a client is a positive one, even if it is with a client who you end up despising and do not want to keep doing business with. As always, when we are conversing about freelancing, positive means that the client enjoys the interactions so much that they are willing and excited about continuing to work with you.

Communicate Effectively

This one might initially seem intuitive, but there are strategies around the way you communicate which can cement you as not only an expert freelancer but an expert communicator.

Keep in mind that you might not be the only one confused about the freelancing process. Your customer might also be inexperienced and will therefore be wanting to be guided by someone who can make the process feel less stressful and more comfortable.

The important thing to keep in mind when devising ways to communicate with your client is that you should be proactive as opposed to reactive in your approach. Even if you are new to freelancing, explain to them your process and what you intend to deliver to them as the product or service you are offering. You can also describe how the platform works for you as a freelancer and the best way for the client to get in touch with you. Ideally, it is best to offer the client more than one way to get in touch with you so they feel that they are connected to you and can reach you at any time which is a comforting feeling for a client. However, not all freelance sites will allow you to do this and will require that all communications be centralized on their platform. In that case, explain to them your response times and how you plan to go about your communication in terms of checking in with progress updates.

The more information you can provide, the better. The more things the client has to guess or be confused about, the more they will be unsure about the experience they are having working with you. Explain the entire process if you can and inform them of what are the steps they need to take even after they are finished working with you; this way they keep thinking about you and the positive experience even after your collaboration has concluded.

Even if your customer is not very communicative, check in frequently with them even if it is just to ask them if they have any thoughts or suggestions regarding the progress that has been made on the project you are managing for them. Do not worry about annoying them with too many questions because at the end of the day, the most important thing for a client is being able to trust a freelancer, and when they see your level of professionalism manifested in your communication, they will be less likely to micromanage and doubt your judgment. Furthermore, it is better to have a customer review your work early and request subtle changes than have them show up at the very end and request a dramatic change that will require that you reconfigure everything that has been done thus far.

If you see that your client has written to you asking for changes, always make sure to respond and then make the changes they are requesting. Many freelancers are quick to address the concerns of the client and become so devoted to making the work as excellent as possible that they forget to inform the client that they have indeed addressed their concerns.

In the instance that the client's views on the work oppose your own, do not think that you have to simply stifle your own opinions and always succumb to those of your client. Doing this does not reflect confidence and at the end of the day, regardless of how inexperienced you are in your niche, you are still probably a lot more capable of completing the job than the client is. Therefore, always be sure to express your opinions in a respectful and professional way but ultimately let the client know that the final decision will always come down to them.

Do not be forceful with your suggestions. If the client says they do not agree with your vision of the project, then move on and make the changes that are being requested.

Keep Things Positive

Remember that you should aim to ensure a positive experience throughout the entire collaboration. Positive does not mean that you do not face challenges or setbacks throughout the process, but that regardless of what comes your way, you always frame it and address it with a solutions-based mindset.

Building upon the concept of being proactive as opposed to reactive in your approach, there is work that needs to be done before the project even begins that concerns the way you will communicate with your client. As a beginner freelancer, it might be challenging to make a comprehensive list of possible inconveniences and issues that could arise, but regardless, be aware of things that could appear throughout the process such as delays, or differences of opinion so that you do not become overwhelmed if they come your way. More importantly, make a plan so that you know how to remedy these difficulties and so you can keep the experience from feeling negative by explaining how each challenge is going to be dealt with to ensure the project does not suffer.

If you are dealing with a particularly difficult client who is not making the process easy for you—and you most probably will encounter a client like this at some point—do not take it personally. The first thing you should do is review your own process to ensure that perhaps it is not your own shortcomings in terms of how the project is being handled that is failing to please the client. When we devote a lot of time and effort into what we do, it can be hard to do this step because we believe wholeheartedly in the work we are creating. However, creating great work and communicating efficiently are two very different things.

Before you formulate a response, audit your communication and see if there was anything that was misleading or could have been the cause for whatever issue arising throughout the collaboration. If you feel that you have communicated efficiently, keep in mind that you are both working toward the same goal of creating the best end product possible. Do not dwell in mistakes, misunderstandings, or disagreements, but strive to forge a way to come to a mutual understanding of what needs to be done to keep moving forward productively.

Keep an Open Mind

Another important consideration relating to positivity is keeping an open mind at all times. If you are a freelancer who is pursuing a niche that is based on a skill or a talent that you are very passionate and proud about, it can sometimes be hard to accommodate the vision of the client.

It is critical to always be aware of the fact that the vision of the client will always come first and therefore you must keep an open mind about how the project will be structured and how it should look once it is finalized.

Do not allow yourself to become too set on one particular way of doing things because your client could at any moment ask for changes that you do not agree with. Moreover, just because the client wants the project to be handled a certain way does not mean that they are right, either. More often than not, you will be right when opposing an idea the client has in terms of quality. However, it is imperative to remember that your job is always to create exactly what the client envisions as the final product, not what you envision it to be.

Don't Lose Sight of the Human Factor

At the end of the day, both you and the client know that you are both handling business and that your interactions are occurring exclusively on the basis that you need to be constantly engaging with each other to get the work that needs to be completed. However, part of your job as a freelancer is to veil that truth as much as you can. Just like you do not want your client to see you just as a means to an end, the client does not want to be treated as nothing more than a paycheck.

Ensuring a positive relationship with your client demands that you constantly communicate a vast array of technicalities that can inherently get in the way of the relationship feeling anything other than a business formality.

Therefore, a freelancer has the sometimes arduous task of balancing the need to constantly be communicating progress or setbacks relating to a project while ensuring the conversation is still friendly. This requirement is hard to accomplish when communicating about business, so do not be scared to talk about personal matters that are unrelated to the project. Your ultimate goal is to create a relationship as opposed to a professional network. Clients are more likely to provide repeat business to freelancers if they feel that they have a personal relationship with the freelancer that surpasses just business talk.

Unlike when delegating a certain project to another company, clients do not get the opportunity to speak with a variety of different people who all work for the same company and are tasked with different responsibilities regarding the competition of a client's project. Instead, clients have no option other than to be in constant communication with only one freelancer. Even if you were to try and keep things exclusively business-related, without expressing any personability whatsoever in your communication, it is inevitable that your client will ultimately create an opinion of you. It is human nature to create ideas of people even if there is very little evidence to support any opinion we may conjure up.

Treat your client like a person and not just someone who will be paying you for your services. Make them feel like you genuinely care about their thoughts and feelings regarding the project and try to emit the same care and passion for the work yourself.

When you feel that it is the right time and the conversation regarding the specifics of the project has slowed down, ask about how the client's day is going. Do not ask personal questions or go into too much detail about your personal life, but make sure you have weekly conversations about things that are unrelated to work.

By not losing sight of the human factor, you make it so your client does not immediately forget about you once the collaboration has been finalized. If you share some aspects of your personal life, your client might remember you when they are just going about their day, which is precisely the kind of experience retention that you want your clients to have at the end of each project so they think of you when trying to find a new freelancer for their upcoming projects.

The trick with this consideration is to be open about yourself and your life without letting yourself get too emotionally involved with the project. Even when you are sharing aspects of your life with the client, keep some healthy detachment from the project so you do not get emotionally overwhelmed if the client makes absurd demands or tries to redirect the aim of the project to a place you deem unproductive.

Learn to Anticipate Their Ideas and Needs by Getting to Know Them

There is a saying that is used a lot in sports that goes, "know your personnel" or "KYP." It is a simple concept but one that goes a long way, especially when it comes to client-facing jobs such as the one of a freelancer.

Another saying that will resonate with any G.I. Joe fan is, "knowing is half the battle." Both these sentiments are true when it comes to devising ways to ensure a positive experience with the way you communicate with a client.

This consideration falls under the idea that we explored earlier about being proactive as opposed to reactive in your approach to how you engage with your client. There is a lot that you can do as a freelancer to nurture a constructive relationship with your client even before the project begins and you have said your formal greetings to the client.

Most freelance platforms will provide a concise but to-the-point biography about your future client. The amount of information that will be made available to you will depend on the platform you are using but most sites provide at the very least a description of what the client envisions for the project and what is their ultimate vision for how they want it finalized.

If you are lucky, the information regarding your client will also provide some personal information such as age, location, and perhaps even interests and hobbies, which are equally as valuable to know.

Before getting started on a specific project, write down the things you feel are most telling about your client so you can structure a general idea of what type of person you think you are going to be dealing with throughout your professional collaboration. Even if you are wrong, you will at least be moving forward with the confidence that you have done your homework and are approaching the task as responsibly as possible.

For example, if you read that your client is older than 60 or that they play guitar as a hobby, you now have two pieces of information which can inform you on the best way to address the person and also some fun and personal topics of conversation that are unrelated to the project. If you read that your client is a teenager, you will not need to address them quite as formally as you would the other client who is of a more senior age.

Being able to anticipate what your client might think will serve you well when facing those moments where you reach an impasse and are unsure of how to proceed with a particular challenge that is not addressed in the client's brief and other similar situations.

If no information is provided about the client on the platform, take it upon yourself to find out what you can before getting started on the project. Commence the collaboration by introducing yourself and clearly explaining the logistics of how your contribution to the project will look like. Be as specific as you can about dates and progress updates, so there is as little left to surprise as possible.

After having done so, ask your client to tell you a little about themselves and what they feel are the main priorities of the work that you are going to be collaborating on. You should also aim to be specific in the questions you ask them so they do not feel that they have to do work just to think of things to share about themselves.

Needless to say that your approach when wanting your customer to share a little about themselves will be different each time. Some clients might be very reticent to converse about anything unrelated to work, which will entail you to either ask them pre-prepared questions or perhaps forgo the questions altogether, and there will be times when you converse with someone who cannot stop sharing things about their lives with you. Clients who cannot seem to talk about anything other than themselves will require a whole other type of patience that you must master.

Types of Pre-Prepared Questions

The questions you ask your client will most likely not be the same each time and do not have to be too thought out. As long as you are respectful of their privacy and do not ask things that are too intimate, the client will appreciate the overall sentiment and interest you are taking, seeing them as more than just a paycheck.

Here are a few examples of questions you can ask your client to get your creativity flowing:

1. How long have you been using the platform? Are there aspects of the platform that confuse you that I can help clarify?

2. What do you think is the most challenging thing about working with a freelancer? What can I do to make this process as smooth and productive for you as possible?
3. What do you like to do in your spare time? Do you have any hobbies?
4. Where are you from?
5. Have you been working at your current company for a long time?

Once you have a rudimentary understanding of how your client thinks, you will be more effective in your work because you will understand how they think and will be able to adjust your workflow accordingly. For example, if you are a freelance graphic designer and you follow up on every milestone in the project with a status update and a check-in with your client, you will be progressively gaining an awareness of how they think. After about three times of your client wanting more call-to-action and more vibrant colors to the work you are presenting them, you will know to write "JOIN NOW" in red and yellow for the next proposal.

Go Above and Beyond Their Expectations of You and the Project

Clients do not remember freelancers who deliver the work that is expected of them, they remember those that go the extra mile and submit something that is truly outstanding in their eyes.

One of the ways to do this is by communicating in the way I just described. Another is reflected by the quality of the work you hand into the client. As important as communication with your client is, you must supplement this with an outstanding result.

If you are a freelance writer who has been given a word count that must be completed by a specific due date, an effective and great way to exceed your client's expectation is to deliver your written content at least 24 hours early. After submitting your work, let the client know that you have submitted it so they are fully aware of how you have done better than what was expected of you. Another way to surpass expectations is to do all the essential editing on the content you have written yourself as opposed to still being writing on the last day and leave all the editing to the editor. There is nothing wrong with doing this, but by going above and beyond you will impress not only the client but the editor, securing positive feedback from both.

However, if you want to go the extra mile with the work you have been tasked with doing, you must ensure that you are prepared to do so by creating an effective plan of how to ensure success before you even start working on the project.

If you set yourself the goal of delivering a project early without going through the necessary preparations to ensure that you can manifest those aspirations, you will ultimately become frustrated at yourself for failing to do what you envisioned. Like the saying goes, "fail to prepare, prepare to fail."

Make a comprehensive work schedule that you must follow in order to exceed your client's expectations. Take into account setbacks and client interruptions so that these do not surprise you on your journey to excellence.

Set and Enforce Clear Boundaries

While you should strive to make your client feel as comfortable and supported as possible, you also need to ensure that you feel the same way throughout the collaboration. The best way to do this is to get a head-start on enforcing the importance of a professional and respectful communication from your client.

Some freelancers fear doing this, but the client will end up respecting you more as a confident and organized professional and therefore trust your judgment more.

There are times when clients might do or say things that are hurtful or counterproductive to the collaboration, and although they might not always be on purpose, it is critical that you do not take a passive role and allow this type of communication to continue.

The boundaries that you have to make clear before working together should also be project-related. Be clear with your client about what they are going to receive from you and what you expect to receive from them. This dialogue can include making it clear how many product revisions the client is entitled to so they do not act bewildered when you tell them they cannot leave any more comments after the ones they already have, and at what times it is ok to contact you and when you will no longer accept work calls or written messages.

Make sure that the expectations you set out for yourself are things you can achieve to avoid making it clear that you were unable to deliver on your promise. With this consideration in mind, do not express to your customer that you intend to deliver your product ahead of schedule or things of the sort because you then put yourself in the position of looking like you were unable to deliver when in reality you did what you were supposed to do by turning in the work on the day it was actually done.

Assert Yourself as the Unrivaled Expert

If you do not count on a breadth of experience as a freelancer, this consideration might be hard for you to enact, but it is still imperative that you do at all times. Even if you feel that you are not an expert in your field, by conducting yourself like you are, will allow you to exude confidence and assertiveness that will not only make the process more comfortable and productive for you but for the client too.

At the end of the day, even if you feel that there are freelancers working in your niche who are more experienced or better suited to handle the particular project you are working on, you must remember that your client also chose you because of what makes you unique. Clients pick freelancers who they feel can bring the needed level of experience and skill to a project, but they also pick freelancers based on their personality which hopefully shines through their profiles. As it has been stated previously, clients are paying not only for the delivery of a product or a service but also for an agreeable and comfortable experience. Therefore, do not underestimate the personality component to the decision-making process every client goes through when perusing through a comprehensive list of clients they could do business with.

When it comes to the things that define who you are and how you engage with others, you are truly the unrivaled expert, so embrace that. To continue with the freelance writer example, clients will undoubtedly look at your writing samples to look at your grammar and readability, but they will also be searching for a voice that they feel resonates with their own or that will provide the tone they want for the content they need to be written.

Therefore, always remember that there are aspects of what your client needs that are reflected in the intangible and intrinsic components of yourself that cannot be replicated. By keeping this fact in mind, you will steer clear from any communication with your client that will reflect doubt or timidness on your part.

If the way you interact with your client does not reflect confidence, the client will be more likely to micromanage and be scrutinizing your actions to ensure that things are getting done the way they want them to be done.

The difficult part about asserting yourself as the expert is being aware that this will entail you sometimes having to say no to the client. When you are unsure of your own freelancing abilities, you are quick to assume everything the client says or requires from you is correct and must be adhered to. As a freelancer, one of the most important things you can do is learn to trust and respect your own voice and intuition when it comes to the direction a certain project should take.

Saying no to a client can be daunting, especially if you are in your first year working in the freelancing field and are keen to rack up as much work as possible. However, showing appreciation for your own skills and experience is crucial, and opposing your client's ideas when you believe will not be beneficial to the progression of the collaboration is something you must do. This consideration does not mean that you should behave defiantly or stubbornly, but that you ensure that your expertise is expressed and recognized throughout the communication.

When saying no to a client, always support your comments and counter arguments with evidence. If you simply reject one of their ideas without explaining why you are doing so you run the risk of coming off as petulant or uncollaborative. Another important thing to keep in mind is to make sure you do not turn saying no into a habit. If you feel that your client is making a lot of suggestions that go against your vision for the project, then it is time for you to reassess the direction the project has to take because it is likely that there is an intrinsic discrepancy between how you view the project and how the client views the project. Don't forget that you are free to oppose certain suggestions about how to get to a common goal, but the ultimate goal will always be set by the client.

Give Yourself and Ask For Feedback

The last thing you must keep in mind when working with a client is to always be thinking of ways to improve as a freelancer and as a client project manager. Regardless of how positive or negative you felt, the collaboration with a client went, always go through the things you felt you did well and the things you need to improve on to ensure the next time you work with a client you can address every point. If at any point you felt that the communication between you and the client did not go as smoothly as you would have liked, investigate the process to find if perhaps this was a consequence of under-preparation on your part or if the brief that was given to you by the client was misleading or underdeveloped.

If you find that there were mistakes made by the client, do not simply write off the situation as something that needs to be improved on by the client. Devise ways where you can help the client do better next time, for example, by making a list of the most important points you feel are reflected in the brief and asking the client to respond if they agree with your priorities.

Perhaps you find that much of the conflict between you and the client revolved around the client asking for changes that severely hindered your time management schedule. Rather than simply hope that situation does not happen again, look at your schedule and find ways to ensure that if it happens again, you have enough time to troubleshoot and go back on the progress that has already been made to satisfy the client's needs.

Lastly, ask the client for feedback on your work. Request from your client that they explain to you what aspects of your collaboration they enjoy the most and which they feel you could improve on moving forward. Do not simply accept whatever your client says at face value, but also do reject a suggestion simply because you initially disagree.

Regardless of how you feel about a certain collaboration, every project is a chance for you to improve as a freelancer and as a client project manager.

Your interactions with your client are an indispensable contribution to your freelancing success. Without generating positive collaborations with your client you cannot forge a freelancing career. Your professional advancement depends on ensuring the clients you work with continue working with you and that your collaborations with them help you network with more people moving forward.

While it is imperative that you deliver the best quality work possible to each client, never forget that forging a relationship with your client is as important—if not slightly more important—than the deliverable itself. To ensure you are offering more than just communication but also invoking a relationship between you and the client, you will have to go beyond the project brief and the preliminary requirements of each project to be proactive in your approach.

In this chapter, we stressed the importance of asking each client for feedback and reviews. This consideration goes beyond simply finding ways to keep improving as a freelancer; it is also one of the indispensable marketing tactics that we will explore in the next chapter.

No matter how productive each collaboration is, you cannot rely exclusively on the complementary word of mouth of each client to get your name out there. Marketing is something a lot of freelancers struggle with for various reasons. Marketing is a critical component of their business model that cannot be overlooked and should be considered a daily and indispensable requirement for them to be successful, regardless of what niche they are working in.

Checklist

	See yourself as the first and final line of defense for every project you undertake. Make yourself responsible and accountable for all aspects of the collaboration with the client and for the creation of the final product.
	Always be proactive instead of reactive with your approach to engaging with a client. Learn as much as you can about them and the project before you begin working.
	Treat every client as though you want to continue doing repeat business with them moving forward. Ask for feedback and review if possible.
	Strike a productive balance between being personable and professional at all times. Also, combine being accommodating with confidence about your ideas and contributions to every project.

Chapter 5:
Marketing Yourself as an Online Freelancer

Content builds relationships. Relationships are built on trust. Trust drives revenue.
–Andrew Davis

The mistake many freelancers make when focusing their efforts on getting started in their niche is that they do not consider the importance of marketing. When it comes to those who are only just entering the freelancing world, marketing should be one of their top priorities.

Put simply, marketing is the act of promoting your business to the world so that it gets attention which in turn allows you to connect with other businesses and individuals that will want to work with you. Marketing has several iterations depending on what industry it belongs to. In terms of freelancing, marketing can take many forms, such as e-mail marketing, content marketing, social media marketing, etc. However, since you will not be marketing a company filled with employees but a brand that consists of only you, it can be somewhat strange to know how to do it effectively without feeling like you are invading your own space. This chapter will elaborate on the best ways to promote your business and why it is so important to do so.

In a regular company, marketing is just another department that oftentimes does not receive as much validation or significance as the other parts of a business, such as the sales department. However, when it comes to freelancing, marketing should not be considered just a component of your job, but the job itself.

The only way you can grow as a professional freelancer is by growing alongside the people you bring into your business to collaborate with. Your success depends on the number and quality of interactions you can rack up in a given day or week. Having a sound and well-developed marketing strategy will ensure that your business is presented in the right channels for the right people, and with sufficient exposure to ensure that enough people become aware of your presence.

One of the main issues when it comes to freelance marketing is finding a productive way to balance working on a client's deliverable while still marketing yourself on a consistent basis and ensuring that your marketing strategy does not remain stagnant but is always evolving. Many freelancers struggle to find the time to market their businesses when they fully immerse themselves in a project and do not want to take focus away from providing the best service to their clients.

It is true that it will always be a struggle to make time to do both things well. The best way to remedy this issue is to have a clear understanding of what are the best ways to market yourself as a freelancer so you do not waste time doing things that, in the long run, will not be profitable for you and so the strategies that you do put into place are as effective as they are time-saving.

Before delving into the best marketing strategies for freelancers, let's look at what are some of the most common struggles freelancers face when trying to create exposure for their business.

Marketing Struggles

Imposter Syndrome

To market your freelancing business or brand correctly, you must exude an image of absolute confidence and professionalism. Your brand image should make a client feel as confident handing you a project as they would feel handing it over to a large multinational corporation.

Often, working hard to create this sense of confidence can feel very contradictory to the normal struggles and doubts that all freelancers will encounter as they do business.

The truth of the matter is that being a successful freelancer is a colossal—but still achievable—undertaking for anyone. Trying to stay on top of all the things a freelancer must do on a daily basis can be overwhelming and lead to moments of doubt and reluctance to continue. The struggle freelancers face is having to address those troubling emotions while portraying a brand image that is completely contradictory to those issues, which can lead to feelings relating to imposter syndrome.

This issue becomes compounded when a freelancer who is already struggling with imposter syndrome is in constant communication with a client who belongs to a big corporation with very large teams and budgets that can make the freelancer feel like they cannot possibly be enough to deliver something the company will be satisfied with.

The way effective marketing can remedy this issue is twofold. A sound marketing strategy will bring you enough work and projects that your experience will quickly increase, leading to an increase in confidence too. The more work you get, the more confident you become in your abilities because you are proving to yourself that you are able to handle the freelancing gig. Secondly, the best marketing strategy is not the one that brings in as many people as possible, but the one that speaks exclusively to the right people. The right marketing strategy should focus on quality vs. quantity. If your marketing efforts are bringing in clients who are not suited to work with you, the experience you may have working with these people could actually hinder your confidence.

Marketing should make you visible to as many people as possible, but attractive only to the ones who are right for you to do business with. If you limit your marketing to only appear in the channels of people you want to work with, then you are limiting the scope of word of mouth. In other words, even if someone is not a good fit for your business, they could still put you in touch with people that are. A good way to look at it is that you should be striving to create a stage big enough for everyone to see but present something on that stage that will only be attractive to those clients that will help you grow as a freelancer.

Time Management

Freelancers find it challenging to make time to handle their client's projects and work on giving their brands sufficient and consistent exposure to attract new clients. Being that freelancers have no subordinates to rely on, they cannot delegate any of these vital tasks to anyone.

When a freelancer begins their professional journey, they usually have a lot of time to accomplish all the things they need to because they are not tied down to several projects if any. Therefore, once clients start coming in and handing the freelancer work, the freelancer is typically unprepared to handle the workload of managing their deliverables and their marketing. If a freelancer disregards their marketing initiatives, they are less likely to get new business once they submit their current project. On the other hand, if a freelancer pays less attention to their deliverables so they can focus more on their marketing, the client will get a less-than-satisfactory product that will reflect badly on the freelancer.

If a freelancer cannot deliver a satisfactory product or service, their marketing efforts will constantly be aimed at undoing the negative feedback and reviews that are going to be received from unsatisfied clients.

Lack of Knowledge

Another important issue regarding freelancer marketing is that freelancers often do not know the right way to market their brand. Even if you quit a marketing job to pursue a career in freelancing, the specifications of freelancer marketing are unique and must be learned before putting yourself out there and trying to get new clients.

Like with most things regarding freelancing, there are strategies you can use to ensure you are portraying a consistent and effective brand image that speaks to your target market.

Marketing Strategies

There are many things that freelancers should learn practically by going through the laborious process of trying to get clients and working hard to get their deliverables submitted on time. However, knowing the best strategies for how to market themselves successfully is a fundamental consideration they must learn before taking the first step forward into freelancing to avoid wasting time and attracting the wrong market.

Personal Network

It is unreasonable to assume that a novice freelancer will have the ability to connect to a multitude of potential clients before they have handled their first project. At the same time, it is challenging to attract clients if you do not have a portfolio to vouch for your work. A way to get clients while not being able to produce evidence of prior work is to tap into your personal network.

Luckily, we live in an age where we are more digitally connected than ever. Unlike several years ago, we can now get in touch with people we have not spoken to for many years who live halfway across the globe.

By getting in touch with people we trust who would be willing to put their trust in our new freelancing aspirations, we can use our connections as a way to give our brand exposure, get positive word of mouth going, and in the best case scenario get our first assignment from someone we trust and will enjoy working with in the first place.

LinkedIn, X, and Facebook are great places to connect with people while searching for someone to lend us a helping hand. LinkedIn allows us to connect with people we do not even know but might be connected to via other people, and who would be willing to help.

Knowing what to post on LinkedIn can be tricky because you do not want to sound desperate when asking for someone to put their trust in you professionally, but you also want to make it known that you are actively searching for work and would appreciate help from people in your network.

LinkedIn

Here are some guidelines on what to post on LinkedIn:

Be Concise but Tell a Story

People do not like to feel like they are being fooled into buying a product and have become very adept at noticing when they are. If what you are trying to do is ask for help, then be upfront about it and do not try to veil your intentions or use deception.

While it is essential that you are direct and honest about your intentions, people are more likely to react to something if there is an emotional resonance component. One of the most effective ways to create emotional resonance is to create a narrative that people can follow and become invested in reading. This consideration does not mean that you have to write your entire life story on LinkedIn to get the attention of people, but make it personable and put yourself and your experiences getting to the place you are in now in the post. For example, you could write about how daunting it was to quit your full-time job after having worked there for several years to pursue freelancing, but that you are equally excited to see how you can turn your dreams of working in graphic design into a reality.

Leave Your Details

If you manage to get people interested in your story and your brand, they will likely want to pursue a website, blog, portfolio, or any other proof of concept you can provide to review the legitimacy and nature of what you are communicating via social media. Unfortunately, the modern attention span has significantly declined over the past decade and people are not likely to spend more than a couple minutes reviewing just one website. For that reason, it is best to provide as many links to your platforms as possible so they can quickly scan through as many as they need to. Even if you do not have a website yet, make sure to make your personal phone number or email explicitly clear.

Explain What You Are Offering

While it is important to mention your personal backstory and talk about more than just business, people need to know what the purpose of what they are reading is. If someone reads your post but cannot understand the point or how they can help, they are not likely to spend too much time trying to figure out something you should have made clear from the start. Be specific about what you are asking from your network and what you are willing to do in terms of taking on projects. If you feel you are not ready to take on high-stakes projects from unknown clients but are simply looking for advice from fellow freelancers, then make that explicit in the post. On the other hand, if you are actively looking for new clients then make a brief but concise list of the services you offer and how you plan on delivering your projects. The more specific you are, the more chance someone reads exactly what they are looking for and gets in touch, whereas if you are too general then it is easy to blend in with the other litany of similar posts.

Have an Online Portfolio

Whether you want to call it a website or a portfolio, the point is that every freelancer needs to have an online presence where prospective customers can go to find out everything they need to know about the person they are considering doing business with. Without an online presence, you are essentially a ghost in the freelancing world. A website does not just exist for the sake of prospective clients wanting to peruse your job portfolio, it is also there for contact details, reviews, mission statement, and brand identity.

A website serves as your hub for all your business dealings and your 24-hour seven days a week salesman. Regardless of what you write on social media or the conversations you have in networking events, everyone will eventually want to see your website. Ensuring that your website is fit for purpose will make all the difference between someone just looking through different freelancers and someone seeing a brand that resonates with them and exemplifies professionalism.

If you do not have enough time to ensure that your website is as professional and attractive as you can make it, either don't get started and save it for later when you do, or make the time. It is better to have no website at all than a bad website. A bad website sends the message to prospective clients that the freelancer is not equipped or interested in investing time and energy into their own brand. If a client sees an underwhelming website, they will immediately think that a freelancer who disregards their own brand image will surely deliver an equally unsatisfying product or service.

The first thing you must do when working to create your freelancing platform is pick the best website host. If you are not adept at knowing how to decide between one website host and another it would be best to seek help from someone more knowledgeable on the matter because once you begin setting up your website with a specific host you are locked in with that selection and it is incredibly hard to change hosts with every passing day; not to mention doing so would incur a great financial strain on your business.

The next thing you must do is select a domain name for your business. Domain names should be simple and be clear about what the business is and what clients can expect from working with that freelancer. Unlike deciding the domain name of a business, freelancers should not veer too far from the recommendation of simply using their name and their niche as the focus of their domain name. For example, if you are a freelancer writer, then your domain name could be johnsmithwriter.com. The mistake several freelancers make is overcomplicating their domain name because they feel it must be on the same level of creativity and thoughtful consideration as every other aspect of their website. The more clear it is that your domain name is the direct path to you and the services you provide, the better.

Google Keyword Planner is a great tool every freelancer should use to be efficient and strategic with the content they post on their website. Using this resource allows you to distinguish which words are being searched for online by your target market when looking for business in your industry.

Your website should strike a balance between depicting who you are and what your vision is for your brand, and reflecting the needs and wants of your market. Ensure that your personality shines through the website because that will create a clear picture of what type of relationship the client can expect to get if they collaborate with you on a project. Your website will also need to be constructed in a way where the client feels that what they prioritize in a freelancer is present all throughout the branding of your page, which you can achieve by leveraging all the information you acquired previously when conducting research on your target market.

If you are struggling to find ways to create and embellish your website, look at the websites of your direct competitors. The idea is not to copy but to find ways where you can improve upon what they are doing and become inspired to put your own spin on what the competition is doing in terms of brand image. Make a list of the things you see that most of your competitors are doing with their sites and find ways to make it your own and even better. Some freelancers avoid knowing anything about what their competitors are doing because they do not want to be influenced by them, but the truth is that you must always be aware of what is happening in your industry. If you do not have a firm grasp of your competitors, you will not know how you can strategically position yourself to keep growing and improving in your niche.

As you grow and develop your freelancing skills and expertise, you want to ensure your website reflects your professional maturity too. Your work portfolio should always be updated with reviews and testimonials, if possible. If you acquire new skills or learn how to automate certain processes or make life a little easier for yourself and your clients throughout the collaboration process, make that clear on the website. Clients like to know that the freelancers they work with are up to date with the latest advancements in the industry and that they can offer them the most modern and smoothest service out there.

Use Social Media Strategically

Social media has become so prevalent in modern society that any business that wants to be profitable needs to have a presence in at least one platform. However, using social media for the benefit of your business is very different to consuming and creating content as a person just scrolling and interacting for fun. The reason why this section has the word "strategically" in it is because it is critical that you do not fall into the social media trap that a lot of businesses do.

As useful and necessary as social media is, it is also dangerous because of how easy it is for people to misuse and lose sight of its purpose in terms of marketing an online business.

Before even making your first post, research what are the best digital marketing strategies for social media in terms of what platforms to use, what is the best consent to post, and what are the best times to post it. You cannot rely on posting content only when you have the time or when something you feel is post-worthy happens.

Devise a comprehensive social media schedule that details at what time of each day you should use social media to stay engaged with your followers and clients. One of the simplest ways of getting an idea of what your social media schedule should look like is to search for tips on Pinterest. Pinterest offers many useful templates for freelancers looking for a simple yet effective blueprint for their social media strategy.

Once you have a content strategy, the most important thing you can do is ensure consistency. Even the best posts will not create the desired effect if they are not followed up with consistent content moving forward. There will always be days when you do not want to post anything but it is critical that you stick to your schedule so your clients always get the sense that the business is moving forward and constantly engaging with its followers.

Make sure to pin your main website to your social media so people can always be redirected to find out more and get in touch with you. If you are using Facebook, LinkedIn, or X, where you can use headers to embellish your profile, make the header one big banner for your website in big and bold letters. Clients will not be able to click on the header but it will give them an immediate understanding of what the brand is and what everything in the social media platform is related to when it is the first thing they see on your profile.

A common misconception is thinking that when it comes to having a social media presence, more is better. While this is not true, the opposite is also untrue. Less is more does not necessarily apply either. Just like you conducted market research to understand who your target market is, you should do the same to understand what is the best social media presence for your business. Generally, it is better to stick to no more than two platforms but every business will be different.

The last consideration is one of the most important. When using social media consistently, most times on a daily basis, it can be easy to lose track of time and not be aware that your usage of social media has become unproductive. Unfortunately, social media has the ability to turn the tables and begin using the user without them even realizing it. In fact, people spend around two and a half hours daily scrolling endlessly through social media without any purpose other than searching for more content to consume. Be consistent with your daily use of social media to promote your brand, but also be cognizant at all times of how you are managing your time on each platform. There is nothing wrong with researching the content of competitors, but set yourself a time limit for how long you allow yourself to be on social media to avoid losing too much time.

Guest Blogging

A great way to get your name out there when you do not yet have a platform to do it yourself is guest blogging. Guest blogging should not lead you to not write your own content and market yourself through your own channels, but as you are starting out, it can sometimes feel like you are screaming into an empty room when you produce your own written content that is not being read by as many people as you would like.

Therefore, a valuable way to market yourself is to reach out to a guest blogger whose target audience is the same or similar to yours and ask to have a guest blogging spot on their platform. Doing this will provide you with added brand awareness and drive traffic to your blog. While this may sound like a simple solution, finding the right guest blog can be challenging, and most bloggers will want to negotiate a small fee for you to use their site.

However, guest blogging ensures added visibility and is a marketing strategy every freelancer should leverage.

Customized Services

You can also market your work as you are creating it. One of the aspects of freelancing work that clients resonate with most is seeing work tailored to their specific needs and vision.

Furthermore, you can adapt your branding to fit the changing needs of your market. Suppose you see that clients are looking for personality and authenticity in their freelancer more than experience. In that case, you can rearrange your work portfolio to not be the key selling point of your services, but rather create short videos or upload lifestyle photos of yourself to better cater to your target audience.

Always Ask for Reviews and Recommendations

In the previous chapter, we explored the importance of asking for feedback so we can leverage every experience working with a client to improve and grow as a professional. In terms of marketing, it is equally important that we conclude every collaboration by soliciting a formal review and recommendation from the client.

Clients gauge what freelancers they want to work with by seeing how other clients have rated their collaborations with that freelancer. Clients also take into account the amount of reviews a freelancer has. Even if a freelancer has exclusively stellar and positive reviews, if they cannot produce enough reviews to demonstrate a considerable breadth of experience, the client might be inclined to look elsewhere for a freelancer. Clients like to create a general idea of what they believe their collaboration with a freelancer will look like and fewer than five reviews will make it hard for them to do so.

Therefore, it is critical that you try and get as many reviews from clients as possible. Even if your collaboration with a client did not go well or if you feel you did not perform as well as you would have liked on a certain project, do not forgo asking for a review. Often, freelancers can be quite critical of themselves and their process when working with a new client, especially if they are just starting out and do not have enough experience in the freelancing industry.

With the aspirations of doing our best and wanting to deliver the most satisfactory service possible to our clients, it can be very easy for us to be very self-critical and over-catastrophize certain moments in a collaboration. Over time, freelancers should work on developing a tough skin and not letting themselves become too disheartened by complications throughout their collaborations with a client. For this reason, freelancers are often surprised to receive stellar and glowing reviews from clients who they felt might have been disappointed or underwhelmed by the collaboration.

If you only ask for reviews from collaborations you feel went as smoothly and productively as you wanted, you limit yourself to being surprised by very positive recommendations from clients who, although might have expressed issues and concerns regarding a specific project, would still highly recommend you as a freelance professional.

However, it is true that you will not always get exclusively positive reviews. There will be clients who will bring up things that they believe you must work on to improve as a freelancer and that is a completely acceptable thing that we must embrace and use to further our professional development. As important as constructive negative feedback is, freelancers should keep those private and only post those that focus exclusively on the positive.

To reiterate what has been mentioned previously, the best way to ensure positive reviews is by focusing on the quality of the interactions. Even if we make mistakes along the way and do not deliver to our clients exactly what we intended to deliver, if our communication is as perfect as we can make it, the client is more likely to focus on the professionalism with which we communicated with them than on the deliverable.

The critical thing to keep in mind is that we cannot become obsessed too much over the quality of the product or service we are being paid to deliver. Naturally, we must always strive to produce the best quality work possible at all times, but keep in mind that what makes a freelancer a professional that clients will want to work with encompasses so much more than just the work that is submitted at the culmination of a project.

If we can reframe every setback that occurs when working on a client's project as an opportunity to improve, and we communicate the setback to the client in a positive and constructive light, the client will likely not view the issue you have arisen to them as a negative thing. Even the most overwhelming of challenges can be prevented from being perceived as a negative occurrence in the eyes of the client depending on how we communicate to them. Therefore, do not obsess over not running into any issues when working on a project with the aim of securing the most positive review you can. Instead, allow the process to flow naturally while staying conscious of the manner in which you communicate with your client and what perspective you are invoking when discussing challenges facing a certain project.

Studies have shown that 77% of clients are more likely to collaborate with a client who has been personally recommended by a mutual connection. Therefore, asking for clients to provide word-of-mouth recommendations is also advantageous. This consideration is particularly important for new freelancers who are relying on their own personal network of contacts to get work. If you know someone who has contact with people who you believe would be great clients for your business, ask them to put in a good word for you when they can. Furthermore, always have something physical that people can look at when hearing about your services. Online websites are critical, but in networking events, it is hard to ask someone to peruse your website to learn more about your brand. While it is critical that you carry business cards, flyers, or any other tangible promotional material with you, it is equally important that you give some to your personal contacts so they can hand them to their contacts whenever they put in a good word for you and your business.

Marketing can be considered to make up 50% of a freelancer's work requirements. After reading this chapter it is clear that marketing your freelancing business involves many moving parts that must be working in harmony, such as the case with business cards that lead to your social media, which lead to your website, which finally direct clients to your personal contact details.

Taking into account the importance of marketing in terms of freelancing, it becomes clear why freelancers must be up to date on the best strategies to use their promotion efforts effectively. Juggling and merging your efforts into successfully working on your client's deliverables and consistently ensuring your marketing initiatives are meeting your goals requires a lot of dedication and hard work.

Dedication, consistency, and tenacity are vital prerequisites for freelancers wanting to make the most of every project to continue growing professionally. These traits are crucial for success and only a small part of the success-oriented mindset that freelancers must be mindful of nurturing with every experience and collaboration. The next chapter will delve deeper into the mental place all freelancers must go if they are going to be successful in their field.

Checklist

	There are several issues that make it challenging for freelancers to market themselves effectively. The main three challenges freelancers face are feeling like they are not experienced enough to assert

	themselves as experts in their field, not knowing how to balance working on a project while promoting their brand, and not being aware of what are the best marketing strategies for freelancers.
	Beginners should read this chapter and learn the best ways to market themselves while not sacrificing their other responsibilities.
	Understand your target market and personalize your marketing strategies to speak to them directly.
	Always ensure your online presence is updated with your work experience and with the latest trends and technology in your sector.
	Make every collaboration count in terms of using its reviews and word-of-mouth recommendations as promotional material for your brand.
	Have business cards or other tangible materials that you can readily hand to prospective clients and people you trust that can direct them to your online presence.

Chapter 6:

The Success-Oriented Mindset of an Online Freelancer

Thus far, we have explored and examined the various disciplines and requirements of a freelancer wanting to excel in their chosen niche. Being your own boss and the face of everything related to your brand is a proposition that is as attractive to freelancers as it is demanding.

A solopreneur needs to be accountable for everything related to their brand. Furthermore, freelancers need to constantly be identifying aspects of their business that might be hindering their success and rapidly think of solutions that can remedy those issues. All these considerations can be taxing and laborious for even the most disciplined person; which is why this chapter will explore the most fundamental requirement for being successful as a freelancer in any niche—the mindset.

Even if you are equipped with an arsenal of the best strategies, tools, and resources, these will not serve you as well as they could if you do not consider the importance of the mindset you invoke when freelancing professionally. The difference between merely aspiring to acquire all the benefits that come from freelancing and those who actually secure a profitable and comfortable lifestyle from their work depends on the quality of their thinking.

The essential thing to remember is that a success-oriented individual will eventually forge or find the resources needed to succeed. Mindset is something that cannot be compared by running an analysis on your competitors or by numerically contrasting it with your previous performance on a client's project, which is what makes it harder to define and keep at the forefront of your considerations. However, although mindset can sometimes be perceived as an intangible, it is nevertheless a profoundly important aspect of a freelancer's guide to success.

This chapter will elucidate the importance of nurturing the right goal-oriented mindset and knowing what are the key personal attributes a freelancer must have if they are to develop their resilience, persistence, consistency, and determination.

The Importance of Having a Success-Oriented Mindset

Having a success-oriented mindset will ensure that you view your freelancing journey in a positive and productive way, which will allow you to make better decisions and view challenges that arise as potential opportunities.

Fostering and nurturing the right mindset will be very beneficial to any person pursuing a goal, but freelancers especially would benefit from knowing more about this mindset because they are the ones who need to motivate themselves and hold themselves accountable.

There are several components to what makes a success-oriented mindset, however, they all relate to the idea of deciding to view things with a positive outlook so that we may continue progressing and not become overwhelmed by setbacks.

Facing your freelancing venture equipped with a success-oriented mindset will make you more productive and will make it easier for you to make faster and better decisions. Freelancers often become overwhelmed when having to make decisions that could potentially impact the future of their business without having any advisors to guide them. Although this chapter will touch on the importance of surrounding yourself with the right people and advisors, freelancers must also learn how to become confident in their decision-making process.

Knowing how to make fast and well-informed decisions does not entail that you will never make mistakes. Remember that the goal is not to always do the right thing and avoid setbacks altogether; the goal is to be as well-informed as possible and be willing to act based on what you know.

Often, the biggest hindrance for a freelancer wanting to be a better decision-maker, which is one of the most fundamental attributes of being a CEO, or a business owner in general, is a lack of confidence.

A success-oriented mindset helps to clear doubt and makes freelancers see things with a more clear and more focused vision.

Individuals with a success-oriented mindset typically are more motivated to achieve their goals because everything that occurs throughout their day is perceived by them as a stepping stone toward their ultimate objective. For this reason, they become comfortable taking calculated risks and working harder than they have previously in pursuit of freelancing success.

How to Create a Success-Oriented Mindset

Understanding Your Priorities

To create a success-oriented mindset, you must begin by being introspective about your purpose as a freelancer. Having a robust understanding of why you have chosen to become a freelancer and what aspects of this career you are most interested in pursuing is fundamental to nurturing the right mindset.

If you know that you chose to freelance as your career because you want to spend more time with your family, then you will know that your decisions should be geared towards prioritizing your personal time at home. Say that you want to become a freelancer because you want to one day set up your own agency. In that case, your decision-making process will inherently prioritize the importance of branding and maintaining long-term client relations over the other requirements of the job.

Goal-Setting

Having goals is like inputting your final destination into your GPS. Without a goal, your successes will not reap the same rewards they would if they were all aligned under a common objective.

Your goals should be challenging enough to ensure that you are working hard but also achievable enough so that you can regularly feel a sense of accomplishment. Your goals should not be too general so that they appear vague and do not give you a precise understanding of what you should be doing each day to meet that goal. For example, if you decide that your goal is to become a successful freelancer, you will need to break that goal down into smaller goal segments that you can achieve every day or every week.

As you begin your freelancing journey, it is important to set goals that you can achieve with the limited experience and resources at your disposal. Furthermore, accomplishing little goals at the beginning of your freelancing journey will instill a powerful sense of accomplishment that will motivate you to keep accomplishing different objectives to chase that feeling.

Something as seemingly simple as defining your niche can be your goal for the day, while having chosen a website host can be your weekly objective. The best way to go about setting goals is to set daily goals each morning but also have weekly and yearly goals that you can work long-term to achieve.

Keep yourself accountable with your goals. As you go through your daily and weekly to-do list, identify what tasks are the ones which are the most time-consuming and therefore require that you discover ways to be more time efficient.

Lastly, write down everything that you accomplished or struggled with throughout the day. Creating a written prompt that summarizes the day is an effective way to tell the brain that the workday is over, and it also helps cultivate positivity as you celebrate your little victories on a daily basis. After enough time, you should have a narrative that depicts your progress week after week, month after month.

Keeping a journal of your progress reminds you that no matter what happens on any given day, you are always one step further from the place you were in the day before. Learn to appreciate every little achievement to ensure a positive outlook on your journey.

The Power of Positive Thinking

By getting into the habit of accomplishing small yet rewarding daily goals, you nurture your self-confidence, which in turn provides you with a positive outlook and attitude. Positivity and confidence go hand in hand and the more you work on enacting one you inherently improve the other as well.

There are several ways to exercise positive thinking. There are people who write down or speak their daily affirmations as a way to manifest their vision of how they want to feel and view themselves, while others practice resilience every time they are faced with a challenge.

The good news is that all of these attributes and considerations are linked to each other. The moment you have an understanding of why you have made the decision to pursue freelancing, you can begin to set challenging yet achievable goals. The more you accomplish the goals you set out for yourself, the more confident you become in your abilities, which rewards you with a more positive and resilient attitude.

Imposter syndrome is one of the main challenges freelancers face when trying to create a positive attitude during their work. Some freelancers like writing down their negative thoughts in a journal and then writing positive responses to them as a way to recondition their brain to see the positive instead of the negative.

Being positive does not mean that you should never feel discouraged or overwhelmed by what you are trying to accomplish. Freelancing requires a lot of hard work and it will be taxing on everyone. Do not feel like you are failing to be a positive person because you are having a particularly difficult day where you are not achieving your daily goals. Sometimes, the only solution to create positivity in your work life is to take a break and step away from the workload.

Visualization is another powerful tool when trying to frame the path that lies ahead in a positive light. Once you have jotted down what your aspirations are, make sure that you can also envision them with as much vivid detail as possible. Knowing what your goal actually looks, sounds, and feels like will make it a much more appealing prospect and one which you will pursue with more enthusiasm because it will feel more real than if it were just words on a page.

Take a Break

Knowing when is the right time to take a step back from work and reward yourself with some time off can be a challenging thing to gauge, especially if you are in the early stages of your freelancing career and are very motivated about doing as much as you can as quickly as you can.

On one hand, you do not want to feel lazy or like you are taking a break when your competitors are still working and persisting through their exhaustion. On the other hand, you do not want your work to suffer because you have worked so hard that it is unproductive to keep going without taking a break to refuel your system and regroup.

Like with most things relating to freelancing, balance is an important consideration when learning when to take a break. Often people think about freelancing as something that awards people the freedom to be able to be adhoc about their breaks without there needing to be any planning involved. While it is true that it is possible to decide to take a break at any given time, this is not the most productive way of going about your holiday planning.

Having a plan for when you are going to take a break is a little bit like knowing what your goals are. If you know when your next holiday is, you will work that much harder as you get close to your holiday because you will want to get everything done on time and earn the break you give yourself. This consideration is an example of the importance of having a routine to help you obtain a success-oriented mindset.

Create a Routine

A common mistake that freelancers make is believing that the freedom that is awarded to them by opting to pursue this particular career is an excuse to not create a schedule or routine for their day. While you do not have to follow the conventional nine-to-five lifestyle of an employee, you should still ensure that you follow a daily routine that works for you and allows you to be as productive as you can.

If you feel you are more creative at night, then ensure that you schedule a time in the evening to do your promotional and marketing work. If you would like to have your Mondays free to be with your family, ensure you get all your work done by a certain time every Sunday.

Just the act of repeating the same action on a weekly and monthly basis creates a sense of comfort that is very advantageous for a freelancer. Not knowing at what time you will wake up or get to work can be very stressful and lead to an uneasy sense of unrest that will make it difficult for you to feel motivated or confident in your work.

Remember that your routine should be made to be flexible so you can troubleshoot in case anything occurs throughout the day that makes you need to move things around.

Routine is not limited to just the things you need to do for work. In this case, routine refers to everything you do throughout your day, even if it has nothing to do with your freelancing responsibilities. Something as simple as the order in which you drink your coffee and read the news can be an important consideration when trying to stick to a routine. Other things that you can fit into your routine are the time you exercise, the time you take a break from working, and the time you start unwinding from a day's work by meditating or watching an episode from your favorite TV show.

The idea behind sticking to a routine that encompasses all different aspects of your day is that after you do the same thing repeatedly for an extended period of time, eventually you do not have to think about what to do throughout your day and you just do it out of instinct. With enough time, you will not need to think about going downstairs to read the news or go for an afternoon stroll to clear your head; you will do them out automatically as if you were on autopilot.

If you do not need to think about going about your personal errands, you will also not need to think about accomplishing your freelancing responsibilities either. The less decision-making a freelancer can have throughout their day when it comes to the mundane, the better. True decision-making should be reserved for more high-stakes decisions as opposed to ordinary considerations.

Staying Motivated

A positive attitude will cause you to see your vision for yourself more clearly, and therefore, make you more motivated to keep pursuing that vision. Motivation is an important contributor to your success, but it is not something that freelancers should become solely reliant on.

Regardless of how positive our attitude is and how precise the goals are that we have set out for ourselves, there will always be times when we do not feel our best. However, this does not mean that we must stop working and desperately try to find our motivation again before continuing with our work.

Your motivation should be something that is so intrinsic within you that you still have it even when you don't feel it. Motivation should not be a fleeting sense of euphoria, but an unrelenting commitment to yourself that you will always find a way to keep moving forward regardless of the odds or the way you feel.

Support System

Surrounding yourself with people who are aware of your journey and are motivated to keep you on track and focused will prove to be a highly beneficial advantage. As important as it is to learn to be autonomous and self-reliant, even the most productive freelancer must know their limitations and how they can be addressed with the help of others.

It is better to select a small group of individuals that you trust to guide and point you in the right direction if you start deviating from the goals you have set for yourself. Many freelancers select a couple of friends or family members to have as their support network during their freelancing journey.

It is important to ensure that the people you select to support you during challenging times are fully aware of what your goals and priorities are. If you are not clear about what you are trying to achieve both short and long-term, your support system is likely to envision something that differs from what you are actually striving to create and therefore not be able to assist you as well as they could.

As advantageous as it is to have a support system to steer you in the right direction during trying times in your career, it is equally important to ensure that you do not become overly reliant on them. Like with most things that are there to support a freelancer on their journey, they can be abused to the point where they become detrimental to the freelancer. There should never be anyone telling you what to do or having to remind you on a daily basis what your responsibilities are. Your support system is just another defense that is there to help you achieve the goals you have set for yourself, but the first and last line of defense will always be you.

Moreover, do not ask too many people to be your support system. Having too many people in your support system is the same as having only one. If you can enlist the help of around two to four people that you trust to be there for you when things get challenging, you will be more motivated, and therefore, more productive.

Seek Guidance

Remember that freelancers must always be students of their industry. Regardless of how much expertise we have in a certain niche, knowing how to use that experience and knowledge to create a career in freelancing is an entirely different discipline.

Moreover, being a freelancer entails that we try to control every aspect of our business and assure ourselves that we are experts in our chosen fields. However, as important as it is to behave in a certain way that exudes absolute confidence in our skills, we must also be aware that there are others who know more than we do and can provide us with a lot of useful knowledge.

Freelancers must learn how to distinguish between the moments where they have to push themselves to continue moving forward, even when the result of their efforts is uncertain, and when to ask for guidance from other more experienced freelancers.

There are a lot of resources that can help a freelancer improve as a professional, such as this book, but it is not uncommon for freelancers to sometimes shy away from asking for help.

When you spend so much educating yourself on an industry and convince yourself that you are capable of accomplishing everything you need to accomplish by yourself, it can sometimes feel counterintuitive to ask for help from someone with more experience, such as a competitor.

Although you are competing with other freelancers doing business in your niche, you should still be able to have an amicable relationship with them and even ask them for advice if you feel they can teach you things which would be advantageous to your business.

Don't Compare

It is critical that you do not compare yourself to other freelancers doing business in your niche as a way to gauge your progress. Comparing yourself can deviate you from the productive path you are on and make you create false expectations for yourself that are not based around your goals but on trying to surpass or do as good as your competitors.

The only person you should be comparing yourself to is the freelancer you were the day before, which you can do by perusing your progress journal that you should be writing in every evening once your workday is over.

Every freelancer will have different strengths and weaknesses, so trying to replicate what a competitor is doing will not be conducive to your development as a professional. Comparing will most likely lead to you feeling demoralized and unmotivated.

Therefore, celebrate the small daily achievements and only focus on your own path without becoming distracted by what other freelancers are doing.

Keep an Open Mind

One of the biggest detriments to success is not embracing a mindset that welcomes change. This consideration is one that is especially important for professional freelancers who have been working in their industry for a long time and become reluctant to contemplate new ways of doing things or thinking about their careers.

CEO of Abbaszadeh Enterprises and recipient of the Youngest Iranian Businessman Award by Forbes Magazine, Reza Abbaszadeh believes in the importance of embracing a mindset that welcomes change and adversity. Mr. Abbaszadeh expounds on this belief by stating the following:

Abbaszadeh presents the notion that embracing a success-oriented mindset inherently opens the door to success. This idea might seem overly simplistic, but it is important to note that cultivating and maintaining this type of mindset requires a lot of effort. Ensuring that you maintain a driven and positive attitude in the face of adversity is something that will require a lot of practice.

It is easy to behave in a success-oriented manner when things are going well but can be hard to do during trying times. However, as Abbaszadeh states, the key is not to try and force things to go our way but to accept struggle as a teaching moment that lets us change and adapt to the needs of the moment. Often, the reason why we struggle for a prolonged period of time when trying to achieve something is that we fail to recognize that it is not the impediment that is the problem but our inability to adapt to it.

If you have spent a long time and have tried various different strategies to make something work in your company without succeeding, it is possible that you need to look inwardly at your business and see if there is anything that needs to change. Keep in mind that there are external forces that will come to challenge our business just to remind us that we need to be open to evolving our brand and business model.

The Neuroscience of a Success-Oriented Mindset

Much research has been done regarding the importance of fostering a growth mindset to achieve professional success. People with a growth mindset tend to believe that intelligence is constantly evolving and flexible, meaning that having intelligence in one area can transfer into other facets of life.

The most crucial aspect of having a growth mindset is the idea of constant movement. People who nurture a growth mindset see their intelligence and abilities as open receptors waiting to digest data and turn it into insights and lessons that will improve the person in character and intellect. Moreover, and possibly the most critical consideration, is that the growth mindset does not shy away from challenges; it embraces them as a necessary component of development, even if the challenge is failing completely at achieving a desired outcome. When someone with a growth mindset does not experience hardship or challenge, they consider themselves stagnant in their development.

Studies have demonstrated that people who utilize a growth mindset are generally more motivated, engaged, and willing to face adversity and take on new challenges, making them more successful in their field. Moreover, according to the research conducted by, teaching high school students about the importance and ways to nurture a growth mindset allowed them to feel more motivated and improve their academic assignments. The research showed that students in the growth mindset intervention group did better in their assignments than those in the control group.

One of the reasons why motivation has been linked to success and the willingness to exert effort to achieve a desired outcome is dopamine. Dopamine is the brain's predominant neurotransmitter that regulates the feeling of being motivated. Therefore, it is argued that believing that challenges and failure are a natural part of life and pursuing something which truly entices someone can lead to elevated levels of dopamine and therefore instill an individual with a growth mindset.

Having a success-oriented mindset requires more than just learning to think differently. The productive habits you can conceive of the need to be implemented every day for success to manifest.

Your thoughts and actions work together and are dependent on the quality of each other. To be effective as a freelancer, you must devise productive ways to view your professional advancement and adapt your actions accordingly. Whenever a challenge arises, it is critical that you understand both how to regard that challenge as an opportunity and take the necessary actions to address it as such. After enough time, the things required to foster a success-oriented mindset will become second nature and you will not need to consciously focus each time on ensuring they are addressed on a daily basis.

One of the more fundamental aspects of cultivating a success-oriented mindset is accepting that freelancers are both professionals and students. The learning aspect of freelancing is essential and should never be disregarded or stopped. Regardless of what niche you are working in, it will always continue to develop and grow to fit the changes in technology and the market. Like the industry, freelancers should strive to also be evolving as professionals while simultaneously addressing the needs of their clients.

Checklist

	Having a success-oriented mindset will allow you to be more efficient with your energy and your time. It also enables you to develop as a professional in a more productive way.
	Enacting a success-oriented mindset means creating a plan for how to be as effective in your job as possible and going about executing that plan every day.
	To cultivate this type of mindset, you must understand why you want to pursue freelancing as a career and write down your goals. You should create a daily routine that takes breaks into consideration that you follow every day.
	Make sure that you are surrounded by people who can further your professional advancement and do not hesitate to ask for guidance when you feel it is necessary to do so.
	Embrace a malleable mindset that is open to change. If you cannot make something work in your business, do not force yourself to swim against the stream, and consider changing the aspect of your business that is not aligned with an external influence.

Chapter 7:

Continuing Professional Development

No matter how much experience you have, how many degrees you have, or how well-known you have become — there is always something new to learn. Don't rest on your past experiences. If you do nothing to improve your skills, you won't stay where you are. –Laura Spencer

As it has already been made clear in previous chapters, freelancers need to manage all the aspects of their business to rightfully assert to their clients that they are capable of delivering services and products carefully curated by expert procedures and processes. The best way to ensure the confidence you present to clients in your professional abilities is to feel assured that you have done everything to stay on top of the latest trends and developments in your industry.

Even if you can provide a comprehensive and extensive work portfolio that brandishes your previous successful collaborations to prospective clients, this will not be enough to create the assurance your future collaborators will need to trust you with their business. Previous success is not an indicator of future success when it comes to freelancing. If you continue to deliver the same outdated services to prospective clients, they will opt for working with a freelancer who has a better grasp on the industry, even if your previous experience is exemplary.

What Is Continuing Professional Development (CPD)?

Unlike in traditional employment scenarios, freelancers do not receive annual performance reviews or professional training activities to help them progress as professionals. The freelance industry offers two ways for professionals to advance; client feedback that helps secure new and repeat business, and CPD.

Continuing professional development refers to the imperative consideration that is especially relevant to freelancers regarding the need to always be seeking new information and educating oneself on the evolution of the particular industry that individual is working within. Professional development can manifest itself in several different ways and should be an essential component of every freelancer's daily routine.

This discipline encompasses various different formal and informal educational activities that anybody, regardless of what industry they work in and even those who are not freelancers, should take advantage of. This chapter will explore the various activities that can be undertaken by someone wanting to enact CPD into their business model and what are the benefits that speak directly to freelancers.

There is an almost endless amount of both technical and soft skills that a freelancer can choose from when looking at taking part in a CPD program. The right skills to focus on improving will depend on each freelancer in terms of their strengths and weaknesses and also on the niche they are doing business in. Like marketing and brand promotion, focusing on continuously growing as a freelancer should be something you devote time to every day. Neglecting to make CPD a staple of your business model will hinder a freelancer's productivity because it will inevitably create more work for them as opposed to teaching them ways to be more efficient with their projects and successful with their client interactions.

Frank C., a financial analyst for Paro Finance says the following regarding the importance of CPD and the opportunities that professionals miss out on by not integrating CPD into their lives, "...unless you change that approach and work on those soft skills and do some of those (professional development activities), then you can charge a higher dollar amount, work less hours and at least be neutral in terms of total revenue, if not grow your revenue".

Frank's quote depicts the use of CPD as a savvy business strategy that can help you charge a higher amount for your services if you go about training yourself the right way. Essentially, CPD can be viewed as an integral component of freelancing because, if executed correctly, it can minimize the amount of hours you work, allow you to be more confident in your client interactions, and make more money with each project.

With the rise in job automation from AI, freelancers need to find ways to set themselves apart from businesses that offer the same niche services through technology by offering services that are more attractive to clients or at least competitive.

Lastly, CPD has no finish line. Even if you feel that you have learned everything you need to know about your niche, you should never stop considering yourself a student of your industry and profession. The needs and tastes of your market will never stop evolving so neither should your development as a freelancer. This consideration is especially poignant for freelancers in the early stages of their careers trying to learn how to get started as freelance professionals.

However, there is also a case to be made about how it is also equally—if not more—important for experienced freelancers to continue having CPD be a staple in their business strategy. Freelancers with several years of experience in their field are more likely to become accustomed and comfortable with a certain routine and way of doing things. This condition can make it increasingly difficult for them to allow their strategies to evolve with time and be malleable. Essentially, the longer you do something that has proven effective for you in the past, the more challenging it will be to let go of that habit and try to adopt a new one.

To avoid this complication arising, always be learning and trying to discover ways to streamline, automate, and improve the way you do business as a freelancer.

Upskilling and reskilling are two components of CPD that, although similar, come into effect in different situations and produce different changes in a freelancer's business.

Upskilling

Upskilling is an important aspect for continuing professional development. The other being reskilling, which we will explore in the next section. Upskilling refers to educating yourself on a subject that you have already learned to improve your understanding of that subject and be able to implement it in more productive ways in your business.

Upskilling is more symbolic of the basic principle of continuing professional development since it embodies the notion of continuing more than reskilling does. Freelancers should constantly be practicing upskilling to ensure the services they are offering to their clients are not outdated and are representative of what an expert in their field would offer.

There are several ways to upskill your area of expertise, such as reading industry publications, attending trade shows, being active in Facebook or LinkedIn groups relating to your field or expertise, and subscribing to video channels that offer regular updates and tutorials on how to improve as a freelancer in your niche.

You can also sign up to receive information regarding the latest webinars or newsletters about your industry to minimize the amount of searching you must do to find ways to upskill your talents. The more you can automate the way you receive the resources that allow you to upskill better. If you are spending more than an hour a day searching for information that can help you pursue your CPD aspirations, you have not yet found a way to seamlessly integrate upskilling into your routine. To ensure you do not spend too much time searching for educational material that can help you improve your skill level, subscribe to newsletters, YouTube channels, weekly or monthly webinars, and anything that allows you to take a backseat and receive the invitations to events you need to continue being a student of your industry.

Reskilling

Reskilling refers more to those individuals who are in need of learning a new skill set as opposed to continuing to develop one they already have.

Regardless of how successful you are in your niche, reskilling can sometimes be a necessity for freelancers who are not finding enough work by focusing on just one skill set and need to invest their time into learning another to amplify their service offering to clients. Reskilling does not necessarily entail that you abandon the niche you are working in, because you can employ reskilling while still upskilling your current area of expertise simultaneously.

There are several reasons why an individual would decide to reskill and learn how to be successful in a different niche. Sometimes the reasons are purely financial, such as the case would be if a freelancer notices a sustained increase in demand and popularity within a certain industry that they feel they could do business in if they learned how to deliver those particular services. Other times, a freelancer might feel that the services they offer clients could be greatly complemented with a similar service that would go hand in hand with what they are currently offering. An example of this would be a freelance videographer discovering that they could make more money and provide a more well-rounded service offering if they also learned how to professionally edit the content they shoot for clients.

However, there are instances when freelancers discover they are either not passionate or profitable enough to continue pursuing the niche they are currently working in and therefore must pursue reskilling and abandon the work they had been doing thus far. This scenario is unfortunate, but it is important to remember that just because a particular niche has not proven to be profitable for you does not mean that you should abandon your pursuit to be a successful freelancer altogether. Reskilling is a productive way of continuing on your path toward freelancing success while attempting to become an expert in a different field.

Sometimes, reskilling does not entail you learning anything about a new niche at all, but rather focusing on improving your soft skills so you can become more adroit at handling client interactions. When it comes to being a successful freelancer, soft skills are just as important as technical skills.

The type of soft skills that you can focus on improving through reskilling or upskilling are time management, teamwork, organizational behavior, public speaking, interpersonal communication, and leadership, among many others.

Every freelancer should look at what soft skills they believe they already have but could do with some upskilling, and which they feel they are lacking and deserve to be improved through reskilling.

Benefits of CPD for Freelancers

Continuing professional development has several benefits for every business professional, but freelancers can especially benefit greatly from introducing and maintaining CPD as a staple of their daily routine. Freelancers can gain an advantage over their competitors by getting more projects done in less time, but also by gaining more knowledge about their niche in less time. Therefore, do not make CPD a yearly or monthly practice, but a daily one. Sometimes all it takes is thirty minutes to read the publication of choice that informs you of everything you need to know about your industry.

CPD allows freelancers to keep their skills and expertise up to date with the latest trends and developments in their industry. Clients who work with freelancers typically have a lot of experience collaborating with independent workers and will be quick to figure out which freelancers are experts in their field and which are not due to a lack of knowledge.

CPD also helps freelancers be more efficient with their work. Sometimes, we can try several different ways to automate or streamline a process that is eating up our time only to figure out that there are already resources in existence that can do much of the work for us. Endlessly trying to manufacture ways to be more productive can actually create the opposite effect if we do not study what the industry can offer freelancers in terms of modern tools and resources that were not available when the freelancer began his career.

Moreover, the more expertise you have in your chosen field, the more complex and demanding the work you take on from clients can be. If your resource and knowledge arsenal is limited, so will the availability of projects you can take on. Generally speaking, the more complex a project is, the more you are going to be compensated. Therefore, CPD creates more opportunities for freelancers who want to begin taking on more complex work to generate higher revenue. Clients who can see complex work in a freelancers portfolio will be quick to believe that they are looking at the profile of an expert in their field, and therefore be more likely to trust you with work that they would only give to freelancers they are willing to pay a lot of money to handle the top-priority projects. Clients will also see your brand as credible and therefore recommend you to others who might be in the market for a freelancer to take on their business.

Lastly, CPD gives freelancers the opportunity to network. One of the best ways to stay updated on the development of your industry is to attend trade shows, conferences, seminars, or even webinars. These events allow freelancers to break free from the isolation that comes with the territory and can become overwhelming at times.

Apart from the benefits of socializing, meeting people in your niche is a great business opportunity, too. Even if you are just attending a webinar, these networking events are an opportunity to network with people who can put you in touch with clients or become mentors of yours who can help you navigate freelancing by sharing with you their knowledge of the industry.

Setting Up Your CPD Initiatives

Before getting started on integrating CPD into your life, define what skills your career path requires you to have to be successful. There is no sense in simply trying to learn as many technical and soft skills as possible if they are not relevant to what you are trying to do as a business professional.

Secondly, define how the skills you already possess compare to the ones that are needed in your industry. Equally unproductive is the idea that you should just pursue CPD without an understanding of what are your strengths and weaknesses. If you are a great communicator and leader but lack the technical knowledge required to excel in your field, it would be unproductive to take a soft skills upskilling course when you should be working to improve your technical skills.

It is also important to note that you will not have time to work on every skill you want to improve on. If you take on too many courses, you will not be able to excel in any of them and will end up only gaining a cursory knowledge of the many things you have tried to learn. Even if you find that you are lacking in several different disciplines, choose up to three soft and technical skills to improve on as opposed to trying to tackle everything you want to learn at once. You can always learn a new skill once you feel you have invested enough time into other areas that were previously lacking.

The next step is to find the best way for you to learn these new skills or understand more about your niche. Just because your peers or other freelancers you know find that reading is the best way for them to continue their professional development, this does not mean that their learning method will be the best way for you to improve as well. If you prefer going to events and being there in person to meet people and engage with the industry, then avoid reading the publications and find a way to participate as much as possible in networking events.

Freelancers need to always be evolving and be aware that the industry will do the same, whether they choose to keep up or not. The learning process is constant. The goal is to always be finding new ways to combine the things we learn about ourselves and our niche with our innate creative desire to be unique in our approach to addressing the new skills and knowledge we acquire.

Checklist

	Make a list of your strengths and weaknesses in terms of soft and technical skills in general.
	Define the most critical soft and technical skills required for your freelancing field.
	Compare both lists and select up to three skills that you will both upskill and reskill to improve as a freelancer.
	Decide the best learning method for you, be it online courses, in-person courses, group activities, etc.

Chapter 8:

What I Have Learned as an Online Freelancer

Every freelancer's experience being a solopreneur will be different. Freelancing is a manifestation of the efforts and creative drive that a person can employ to become the leader of their professional lives. Everybody's reasons for deciding to pursue freelancing will be as different as the life they are able to create by making freelancing a profitable and enriching career.

My experience as a freelancer has taught me a lot of important lessons that I wish I would have known before getting started on my journey. I am excited to share with you the lessons that were paramount to my success, so that you may have a slightly smoother transition into a life of professional autonomy.

I have divided the things I have learned throughout my professional journey into ten crucial points. There will be points that will speak more to one freelancer than it does to another depending on their personality and on the areas of freelancing that they are struggling more with.

Do not feel obligated to enact all of the tips I will share with you. If you are someone who has already begun their freelancing journey, you might have an easier time understanding what lessons resonate louder with your experience. If you haven't gotten started but are excited about pursuing a life in freelancing, you can also try out the things I recommend to see if they work for you but feel free to go your own way and test out your own way of doing things.

There is no blueprint for freelancing, and if there ever was, it would only apply to the person who devised the blueprint. Test out different methods, take advice from people who are more experienced, and forge your own path with courage, conviction, and discipline.

Here are the 10 most important things I learned from being a freelancer which can help you achieve success.

8 Things I Learned From Working as an Online Freelancer

Personal Branding

One of the most important lessons I acquired was that it is imperative to have an online presence to promote your products or services as a brand. When I first started freelancing, I was very interested in speaking to clients and explaining my professional journey and what I could offer as my services.

This approach was good in that I included my story into the pitch and added an aspect of friendliness to networking, but I was failing to give my business credibility.

I later learned that you must do more than simply promote yourself, you have to promote your services as you would an entire company. While you are the only employee of your freelancing business, it is important that you brand your services in a way that makes clients feel like they are getting an entire team to work on their projects.

From the first day I started working as a freelancer, I became very active on LinkedIn to gradually build my brand on a daily basis. This was one of the best decisions I could have made at the early stages of my career. By being active on LinkedIn, I was able to network with industry leaders, get advice from people working in the same industry as me, and learn how to build a brand from reading articles. The best part was that I could do all of this every day for free.

I began my freelancing journey as a content writer, which is why it was easy for me to leverage the many resources that LinkedIn has to offer freelancers. The first thing I would do every day before I manage the projects of several clients, would be to write down my thoughts and experiences relating to my industry on LinkedIn. When I would do this sporadically, it helped me to clear my thoughts and connect with like-minded individuals. Once I turned this practice into an indispensable staple of my day, I began getting regular inquiries from interested prospective clients in my inbox.

Once I saw the benefits of creating my own content on LinkedIn, I doubled down on this practice and quickly discovered that I was building my professional reputation online by doing so.

The lesson here is to invest in your online presence to expand your branding opportunities. You do not need to hire an expensive marketing firm to promote your brand; sometimes all it takes is a couple of hours a day to sit down and write down your thoughts about the industry you are in. Whichever way you decide to announce your freelancing presence, do it regularly as part of your daily routine and always engage with people who comment or like your posts.

Be Unique

During the early stages of your freelancing career, it is normal to investigate what other freelancers are doing to try and get a sense of what you should be doing. There is a lot of uncertainty and moments of just idly waiting for work involved with freelancing, which is something we will touch on in this chapter, too.

Not having a boss or a guideline to tell you what you should be doing can be intimidating, which leads many freelancers to try and replicate what their peers are doing in their respective fields. While it is ok to get inspiration, motivation, and ideas from other freelancers, it is crucial that you find your own path.

The first step should be observing. Observe how other freelancers market their businesses, handle their online presence, and manage their niches. The second step should be to experiment. Do not feel like what you do during the first couple of years into freelancing will be indicative of what you continue to do for the rest of your career.

It is ok to make mistakes and try out business strategies that you eventually abandon after discovering they are conducive to your success. The critical thing to remember is to always keep a record of what you have done so you do not repeat your actions and can have a robust understanding of how you got to the stage you are in.

Finally, decide what works best for you. If it so happens that what another freelancer is doing also works for your business, then great; the important thing is to not blindly imitate someone and expect you to achieve the same success they have without trying it out yourself.

The lesson here is that there is no benchmark for freelancing. The only way you will be successful is by doing things your way. Discovering your path to success can take time so be patient and proactive. Do not become restless but rather use the time you have wisely to experiment and make a note of what are the things that work best for you.

Mindset

Cultivating the right mindset for freelancing is one of the most advantageous things I started doing once I realized the importance of behaving like a leader. The mindset of a freelancer can be their greatest ally or enemy depending on how much control you exert over it.

If you have left your "safe" job to pursue freelancing, it is more likely that your mindset will not yet be adjusted to fit your freelancing needs. It can initially seem counterintuitive to learn how to be an effective leader when you become a solopreneur, not managing any subordinates or a team because you are the only person involved in your business. However, to ensure your mindset is geared towards being a successful freelancer, it is important to understand that freelancing is *not* a job.

While it is important to strike a productive work-life balance, freelancing should be regarded as a way of life. You cannot achieve success as a freelancer if you have a 9 to five mentality, where you disconnect from your brand the minute you power down your laptop.

It is beneficial for you to see your interactions and activities throughout the day as an extension of your promotion initiatives and your desire to learn more about the industry. If you meet someone who you believe can connect you with potential clients, be ready to pitch your business to them in an informal way so you do not become annoying but also seize the opportunities around you. If you encounter someone who works in the industry related to your niche, ask them questions that you feel could help them have a deeper understanding of your target market and how to promote your products or services to them.

The key takeaway is to remember to be the CEO of your brand. Be emotionally invested in the growth of your business and hold yourself accountable for all your decisions and actions. Leaders have the most knowledge out of everyone in their company, which makes them fast and strategic decision-makers. Ensure you are as knowledgeable as you can about your niche and embrace every opportunity you see to improve your brand and your position as an online freelancer.

Braving the Unknown

Regardless of how much you master your mindset and your daily routines to make yourself as productive as possible, if you are not working, you are not advancing. This fact can be one of the most frustrating and demotivating aspects of getting started as a freelancer.

The unfortunate truth is that sometimes finding work is out of our hands and the only thing we can do is to wait and be patient. The pandemic taught us that there will be times when it will be challenging to connect with businesses, but if you adjust your business model to address the times, you can actually find a way to leverage every situation.

There is no secret formula to finding clients. Even if you are doing everything right, it can still take a long time before you embark on your first project. Becoming too easily disheartened can be a detriment to your success as a freelancer, therefore, exercise patience during uncertain times is paramount.

Freelancing requires dealing with uncertainty, sometimes for a prolonged period of time, which can be stressful. Not knowing how much money you will be making next month can lead some freelancers to question whether they are doing the right thing in trying to be professional freelancers. In fact, the uncertainty leads many freelancers to quit and return to their old jobs working as corporate employees.

As disheartening as this is, I admit that I too contemplated quitting freelancing every day for the first three years. Even when I manage to get clients and secure enough income, I would then worry about whether I would be able to produce the same success in the coming month.

What some people forget is that even "safe" jobs are not really all that safe. There is always the threat of being fired or the company closing. The best advice I can give is to assure you that it is normal to be worried and to feel like the future is uncertain. Rather than convincing yourself that soon everything is going to be ok and that in a short amount of time, you will become a thriving freelancer handling several projects, learn to embrace uncertainty. Allow uncertainty to come into your life and rather than letting it cripple you, find ways to use your time productively to keep growing your business.

Just Do It

Some freelancers are very gunshy about getting started because they feel they have to first spend several years learning about their niche and target market before making a single business move. While it is important to constantly be educating yourself as a student of freelancing, you will never get anywhere in freelancing unless you take action and take risks.

Even if you know everything there is to know about the theory behind freelancing and your niche, there are things that can only be learned by experiencing them firsthand. Furthermore, I can tell you that even after many years of working as a professional freelancer, you never feel ready. Every freelancer will always live with a healthy level of doubt that can be used to drive their passion. Do not let that doubt deter you from being courageous and moving forward into the unknown.

Balance Is an Illusion

When I first began my freelancing journey, I had an idea of what I wanted to become after having completed several years as a professional freelancer. One of the things I envisioned for myself was getting to a place where I could finally relax and rely on a constant influx of projects and a steady workflow. However, one thing that would have saved me a lot of unnecessary struggle and heartache is the realization that freelancing is different from other professions in many ways, one of the most significant ways being that you cannot count on there being balance in terms of work.

Even as a professional freelancer who can sustain themself and their dependents on just freelancing, there will still be times when you have so much work to do that you struggle to get it all done in time, and other times when you have no active projects for over a month. Rather than becoming disheartened and believing that this lack of balance is an indication that you are failing at your career, understand that this is part of what you sign up for when deciding to become a freelancer.

The earlier you learn to not become overwhelmed or distraught when you do not have enough work to do, the better. Often, new freelancers become so worried that they are going through professional dry spells that they begin doing everything they can to get in touch with as many prospective clients as they can in a rushed and uncalculated manner. Cold-emailing and browsing job boards is a productive way to get clients, but if you are doing it without giving it any thought and just as a means to assuage your concerns, you are likely to not be putting too much focus into the message you are sending across and into who you are contacting.

Going about getting in touch with clients should not be done without being very meticulous about who you contact and how you message them. At first, it might be hard to accept the fact that when it comes to working with clients, it is more about quality than quantity.

The best advice I can give related to this issue is that freelancers must remember that working with clients is only one aspect of their job. If there are times when there are no active projects in your day, use that time to improve your marketing, online presence, branding, and networking responsibilities. You can also use that time to continue developing as a professional. See your spare time as a resource that can help you grow and improve your company and your knowledge of the industry you are working in.

Furthermore, do not try and get too much done at one time when handling several projects at the same time. While it is true that freelancers need to be working on their client's projects, continuing to develop professionally in their field, acquiring new freelancing knowledge and skills, handling their marketing and networking responsibilities, there will be times that they will need to prioritize some responsibilities over others.

Ideally, a freelancer will have enough time to address all the aspects of their business, but there are also times when attempting to do so would be counterproductive and hinder the quality of their work. If you find that you have too many active projects on your slate for a given month, it is ok to let your marketing and networking responsibilities take a back seat for the time being until you free yourself of so much work.

The main thing freelancers need to keep in mind is that their schedules are likely to fluctuate. It is essential to have a routine and that you stick to it, but also be willing to make changes in the moment to ensure that you can exercise complete focus on what you need to prioritize.

Ensure You Have a Financial Buffer

The unfortunate reality is that there will be times when you will not make as much money as you need or expected due to a lack of projects. As uncomfortable as this reality is, freelancers need to be prepared to continue being productive while not being able to invoice clients for their work.

Having a three to six-month financial buffer can offer you a lot of the peace of mind you will need to continue being productive in your work. If you are constantly stressed and anxious about the lack of funds, you will not be able to focus on the tasks at hand.

Moreover, freelancers who are just getting started should try to find a way to lower their cost of living, at least for the first three to four years of freelancing. This consideration does not necessarily entail you doing anything drastically different in your life, but just finding ways to spend less money each month.

Practice Quality vs. Quantity When It Comes to Clients

Working with bad clients can have a very negative impact on your productivity. When you are starting out as a freelancer, it can be challenging to contemplate the notion of saying no to paid work, and at first, it is ok to accept work from clients who you may feel will not be the most collaborative of people.

During your first years as a freelancer, working with bad clients can be a teaching moment where you learn what are the things you should avoid and what are the signs that you are about to engage with a client who will not be productive in your work.

However, moving forward, it is better to enact a quality vs. quantity approach to finding clients. Good clients are the ones who are responsive, respectful, transparent, engaging, and honest. Good clients will make you feel confident and excited about working as a freelancer. Bad clients will have the opposite effect, where they drain you of your energy, and focus. Moreover, taking on bad clients deprives you of the opportunity to work with good clients who could be waiting to work with a freelancer like you, but cannot because you are currently taking on too many projects.

If you focus exclusively on quantity and take on clients who will not be effective collaborators, you are liable to lose out on the very things you were hoping to get from ensuring you had several projects at one time. Bad clients could refuse to pay you or sporadically change the deadline to one that you cannot meet. Bad clients can also be uncommunicative and last minute deny what you are proposing to them. There are many reasons why bad clients can not only unnecessarily drain you of your energy but also deny you the compensation you deserve.

Knowing the right type of client for you will take time and experience. Before you can create an understanding of what a good client is, you must first experience a bad client.

The essential thing to keep in mind is to not let bad client interactions demotivate you from continuing on your freelancing journey. This consideration is very much related to the idea of balance that we discussed earlier. The early stages of a freelancer's career will be filled with both very positive experiences and very negative ones. Always ensure that you are learning and extracting insights from every collaboration so you can cement a clear understanding of the type of client you want to work with.

As you develop your freelancing skills, you will create a narrative entirely on your own based on the challenges you overcame and the strengths you acquired. However, the best way to get started is to expose yourself to the experiences of others so you can get an idea of what awaits you and how you should prepare yourself to meet the opportunities on the other side of the struggle.

Everything you need to know regarding your prospective journey into freelancing has been explained, and all that is left to do is to recount the most poignant points and considerations before you embark on your journey.

Checklist

	Be prepared for times of uncertainty by focusing on your other responsibilities and by having a financial buffer.
	Learn what type of client you like to work with and say no to clients who differ from that vision.
	There is no such thing as being "ready." Embrace the fact that you are going to make mistakes and get started. Be proactive and do not wait for the moment when you feel like you have enough knowledge to be a professional freelancer.

Conclusion

And thus concludes another guide from Change Your Life Guru. As always, keep this resource with you and use it whenever you need the support or knowledge that can give you the very helpful boost you need to claim the life you deserve and can manifest.

Everyone has a dream, but not everyone has the courage to valiantly blaze a path that leads toward making that dream a reality, and fewer people have the resources available to them to make it happen.

When it comes to freelancing, one of the most important resources is information and preparation. You are expected to stumble along the way, but with this guide, you will stumble forward and upward, at least. This guide will be an indispensable asset to your success as you learn to harness your efforts and thoughts productively by knowing where the opportunities lie so you can seize them and use them to grow as a freelance professional.

Making the decision to become a freelancer can be as exhilarating as it is daunting. This emotional rift can follow you throughout the entire process once you begin discovering the lucrative rewards of being a freelancer but also the sometimes overwhelming challenges of going about it as productively and effectively as possible.

Although there are many considerations and moving parts to this rewarding journey, the only way to go about it successfully is to enter it with the knowledge required to avoid the common pitfalls and to make the best of the opportunities that are out there for anyone wanting to establish themselves as thriving solopreneurs.

Throughout the book, we have explored the most crucial considerations that you must have if you want to stand out in your field and make the most out of your time and every collaboration with clients and other freelancers. As we discussed in chapter six, the right mindset makes the difference between a freelancer who becomes overwhelmed with the arrival of setbacks and someone who is prepared to convert any challenge into an opportunity to develop their skills and experience.

The right mindset is key, but even someone with the most focused and productive mentality will still need to push themselves to their limit to make the best out of the amazing opportunity that freelancing offers to everyone. This book does not suggest that there are any shortcuts to securing freelancing success because there are none, just like there are no secrets to success either. However, there are ways of maximizing your time and your efforts to ensure that everything you do is constructive and working with you as opposed to against you, which is a concept we explored in chapter one when discussing the importance of swimming with the current as opposed to against it. Surely there are individuals who can achieve success by swimming against the current, but they will not be as effective with their time as those who are equipped with the knowledge necessary to use the opportunities that are readily available to everyone who knows how and where to find them.

Freelancing does not discriminate and therefore it can be pursued by anyone, which is one of the things that makes it so attractive to people looking to use their talents and expertise as a means to forge a better and more autonomous life. Every person's process to make the best out of their freelancing journey will be different since no one person shares the same weaknesses and strengths. Learning the tools and strategies described in this book will only be useful to you if you can create a firm understanding of yourself.

Before doing anything to establish yourself as a freelancer, remember to take an inventory of yourself and your aspirations relating to freelancing. Make a list of the reasons why you think freelancing is something worth pursuing and what you envision for yourself in the future as a professional freelancer. Identify what you consider are your strengths and weaknesses, but always be aware that these will change as you discover what is required to succeed as a freelancer.

Once you examine yourself introspectively and determine the reason behind your decision to pursue freelancing, you can move on to the next step which is defining your niche.

Some freelancers might feel that they do not need to go through this step because the order of events in their decision-making process begins with already having a niche clearly defined. If you are an individual who is passionate and experienced with a certain discipline, hobby, or talent that you want to make into a business, then you might feel like there is no need for you to look at information regarding niches. While it is true that you should invest your freelancing efforts toward something that you are very skilled in, there are a lot of benefits to researching different niches, such as discovering ways to combine your niche with another that is equally as interesting to you. As was mentioned in chapter one, there is nothing wrong with combining niches into your business structure but avoid trying to become a master at too many things. Clients are more interested in working with an individual who is considered to be an expert in a certain field than working with someone who markets themselves as a "jack of all trades."

If you feel like you want to work in more than two niches, understand that while this is ok to do, it will be harder for you to increase your skill level at the same rate as someone who is working under two or one. And to reiterate what was explained in the first chapter, if you do decide to combine niches, it would be more advantageous to you if they work in harmony and belong to the same industry. An example of this would be deciding to offer freelancing services as both a content writer and an editor, or a videographer and a video editor.

Once you have completed the step, your next task is to define your target market. Knowing how to find your target market requires researching the market in terms of potential clients and also understanding who your competitors are. After executing the recommendations in chapter two, compare your competitor analysis to your target market research to understand which clients you feel would be best suited to do business with you.

Knowing who are the people you are aiming your brand toward is one of the most fundamental steps to defining your marketing strategy.

As we progress through the required steps for freelancing success, do not forget to be patient with yourself and the process. Do not be too hasty to see your hard work manifest itself. Making your presence and your brand an established entity that consistently manages new business takes a lot of time and hard work. However, do not feel that the time it takes to begin collaborating with clients is time wasted. Something this book stresses a lot is the importance of being productive with your time and knowing how to leverage the time you have to your advantage.

One of the best uses of the time you will have when starting out on your freelancing pursuit is marketing. In chapter four, we explored the vital importance of constantly being on top of your promotional responsibilities as a staple of your daily business strategy. Considering that knowing how to balance both working on your deliverables and staying consistent with your marketing initiatives is one of the most challenging aspects of freelancing, focusing most of your efforts on marketing when you still do not have projects to work on would be an effective way to use the time you have.

The way you manage your marketing initiatives defines your positioning statement within your industry. You should ensure that the image you are portraying via your branding is equally reflective of what makes you unique as a person, and also what your clients are looking for when searching for the right freelancer to take on the work they have available.

Remember the importance of keywords. Using Google to get an in-depth understanding of what words your target market is using to search for freelancers will give you a competitive advantage when devising ways to create your main website and social media strategy.

Social media is a powerful tool when it comes to free marketing. It has the potential to reach a global audience without incurring upon you any financial cost. However, always remember to ensure that you are the one using social media and not the other way around. The statistics depicted in chapter five show how easy it is for someone to fall into the trap of thinking they are being productive but really are just endlessly scrolling through content that, although related to their niche, is not providing any useful information. This consideration is especially true for freelancers who must ensure that they are consistently on social media to promote their brand regardless of time constraints or reluctance to do so.

Freelancing is a pursuit that you must constantly be working at improving and evolving. Every experience and every connection you make can be used to grow as a professional as you learn how to network and about the development of your industry. While it may seem daunting to consider freelancing a way of life as opposed to just an occupation, I find that concept exhilarating.

Freelancing awards creative and passionate individuals with the opportunity to showcase their talents to the world and get compensated for them. Moreover, with every project or collaboration, you become better at doing the thing you love. If you are lucky enough to find the right niche for you and determine who is the right market to target, you can secure a profitable and enjoyable way of life that surpasses all your initial expectations.

Summary: The Importance of Taking a Break

Throughout your continuous pursuit of freelancing excellence, always remember to take a break when you need it. In the same way that it is important to remember that you are the only one who will be accountable for the work that needs to be done, you will also be accountable for recognizing when it is time for you to take a step back and regroup. Doing so will be beneficial to you personally, and also for your business.

Freelancing requires that we manage every aspect of our business on a consistent basis. Your brand will only get more exposure as time passes if you are continuously connected to the evolution of your industry and how your direct competitors are adapting to fit the changing needs of their clients. The mindset required to split your focus between the work that needs to be done presently for clients while always acting as a market researcher can drive freelancers to work so hard that they become unaware when they need some well-deserved respite.

It is better to be well-prepared for the eventuality that your efforts become counterproductive to your results due to exhaustion or burnout. As chapter six expanded on, it is advantageous for a freelancer to have someone who can act as their support system and their guiding light throughout their process.

Freelancers do not have coworkers who they can rely on when leaving work to unload their stresses or to share their struggles which can be one of the biggest challenges of freelancing, along with loneliness. Freelancers should always be accountable for their work but having a trusted person who has their best interest at heart can be a very valuable resource when trying to secure professional longevity.

However, it is important to recognize that not every freelancer will have access to someone like this during their work life. Learning to be accountable for your mental health and well-being will be something you will need to be constantly aware of and learn how to manage as you go. There are aspects of freelancing that cannot be taught beforehand but must still be recognized when they occur. Always be aware of the areas of freelancing that you struggle with most and that you believe you might need to work on improving to streamline your processes, but also to ensure you do not burn out and become unproductive.

Some freelancers designate an hour every day to focus exclusively on themselves and disconnect from anything relating to work. There are others who find it more beneficial to designate a certain week or couple of weeks each year to go on holiday, which gives them something to work for and look forward to during those late nights working hard even during weekends.

Summary: The Importance of Having a Work Plan

The freedom that is awarded to passionate individuals by freelancing is something that should be leveraged to make the most out of your time. The most productive way to approach your autonomy is to ensure your work schedule is as comprehensive as you can make it. Some freelancers believe that the freedom they have working as freelancers gives them the liberty to be sporadic and adhoc about when they choose to work and when they decide to work on a certain task based on how they are feeling that particular day.

While it is important to learn how to recognize your own limitations and fluctuations, freelancers must always strive to be working under a regimented schedule that is based on their priorities and time constraints regarding their personal life. Working with the knowledge that you are guided by a schedule devised by you beforehand that takes into account all aspects of your freelancing responsibilities can provide a lot of comfort and help you accomplish your tasks more productively.

Do not feel like your schedule can never be subject to modification. At first, the more your schedule changes the more you are learning about your own process and what aspects of your day need to be adjusted for you to be more efficient.

Perhaps you have created a schedule that determines that mornings are going to be designated to marketing and afternoons to try to get clients. If you test this schedule for at least a couple of weeks and feel that you are more creative in the evenings but more willing to converse with potential clients in the morning, always feel free to modify your schedule as needed. However, as stated, ensure that you give yourself at least a couple of weeks to trial your original schedule to ensure that the things you feel are not conducive to your productivity are not simply related to specific situations of one particular week.

Moreover, there are going to be situations where you feel your schedule has been modified to perfection to make your hours as productive as possible, which will make you very reluctant to ever stray from it. Sticking to your work plan is critical to your professional success, but as with most things relating to freelancing, it is essential that you know how to be balanced in your approach. Regardless of how hard we work on devising the most productive work plan, we must always be prepared to troubleshoot in the eventuality that something in our personal or professional life arises that demands our full attention.

If we become too dependent on the rigidity of our work plan and oppose any deviation from how it dictates we should organize our day, we are likely to miss out on advantageous opportunities that can arise any moment and that we should meet with open arms even if it means not sticking to our schedule.

Summary: The Importance of Client Interactions

The way in which you interact with a client will be very representative of how your business evolves and gets more exposure. A freelancer should view their collaborations with clients as another aspect of their marketing efforts. If you can provide a satisfactory service to a client, that interaction has the potential to lead you to gain access to a larger network of professionals who will, either by word of mouth or by reading your reviews, want to do business with you.

Even if you have an underwhelming client interaction, which you feel involves conflict, or perhaps interactions on your part that you wish you could take, do not hesitate to ask for feedback and for a review. What you show on your personal website in terms of reviews will always be up to your discretion, but every collaboration should serve as a learning experience as well as a marketing strategy.

Often, freelancers who do not yet have much experience collaborating with clients can be overly critical of themselves and think that an interaction was more negative than it actually was. If you have not worked on enough projects with clients for you to have a reasonable gauge of what a good client interaction looks like versus a bad one, you might be quick to assume that a normal setback is reflective of poor performance on your part. This issue is compounded when you consider that they might be dealing with the issue of imposter syndrome which we touched upon in chapter five.

Imposter syndrome is a normal consequence of being an aspiring freelancer trying to learn about the niche they are working in while also learning about themselves as freelance professionals. Freelancer marketing requires individuals to assertively announce themselves as unrivaled experts in their field to attract the business of prospective clients. Considering that aspiring freelancers must begin their professional journey by performing a comprehensive study on their competitors and how they are performing in their industry, it can sometimes be daunting to consider the notion that we are supposed to be competing with experts who have more experience in their field than we are.

The important thing to remember is that there are a lot of freelancers who call themselves experts who are really in the same position we are in, and they are simply portraying a brand image that is intended to demonstrate a level of authority that is needed to succeed in the business. Therefore, do not let yourself feel like an imposter, and be diligent with reminding yourself that you are deserving and capable of being an excellent freelancer.

Imposter syndrome has the potential to be one of the biggest hindrances to having productive client interaction. If a freelancer has a constructive experience with a client but is demoralized by a few setbacks, their imposter syndrome might lead them to not ask for a review that, in actuality, could have been filled with positive and glowing praise for the collaboration.

Furthermore, imposter syndrome can get in the way of our confidence. Regardless of how much experience you have as a freelancer, your communication should always show confidence, without coming off as arrogant. Exuding confidence will allow the customer to trust your judgment more because you will be communicating with them in a way that shows that you are knowledgeable on a specific subject and are willing to defend your expertise during the collaboration. Clients like working with a freelancer who is open to their ideas but is equally unafraid to express and defend their own. A professional and balanced communication of this kind generates respect from the client's side, which is an important thing to have with every project.

Lastly, chapter four touched on the importance of being proactive as opposed to reactive, something that is crucial to the responsibilities of a freelancer and especially poignant in terms of client interactions.

Learn as much as you can about the project you are about to undertake and also about the client you will be working with. Clients want to feel like they are getting the service they want even more than they want to get handed a perfect deliverable. One of the best ways to make your client feel comforted and show them that they can trust you is by making them feel like you understand their vision for the project.

How much information will be available to you via the platform you are working on will depend on the site you use. Usually, every freelancer is given access to a brief that describes the overall goal and idea behind each project. This document is the first thing they should carefully peruse and make note of the most important aspects relating to what the client envisions for the deliverable.

If the brief does not provide information about the client, set up a quick call before getting started to ask the client questions about themselves and about the project. Do not limit the scope of the conversation only to talk about work. Ask questions about their personal life so they feel that you do not see them as just a means to another paycheck. Prepare your questions beforehand and be wary of asking anything too personal because that can make the client feel uncomfortable.

Some freelance platforms do not allow for there to be any client and freelancer communication outside of their site. This will make proceedings slightly more arduous but you still have the opportunity of putting your best foot forward by constantly checking in on the site and making sure that you are responding to all their messages at least within 24 hours of them writing them.

Summary: The Importance of Picking the Right Platform

There are several freelancing platforms that gauge whether a freelancer should be promoted to a higher tier on their website depending exclusively on the reviews they get from clients. As we explored in chapter three, these types of freelance platforms are an advantageous training ground for new freelancers who need to work on their marketing skills and have their interactions with clients supported by professionals who are always ready and willing to advise on how to improve.

By working in a freelance platform that requires you to perform well in terms of client interactions for you to be promoted and grow within the company, you are learning a crucial component of what it takes to be a successful freelancer.

Deciding what site to use to conduct your freelancing work is one of the most important decisions freelancers can make when getting started in their careers. As we explored in chapter three, there are many options, but the two main alternatives that freelancers can pick from are freelance platforms and job boards.

Freelance platforms usually offer a more supportive and active community of freelancers and administrative people whose job is to connect freelancers with clients. The people who manage these platforms also ensure that every project that is posted by a client falls under the same regulations and specifications to ensure that all freelancers are awarded the same opportunity to succeed.

The type of specifications these platforms demand from clients is that all projects include the same information in their briefs, so freelancers have enough information to go by when working on a project. Clients must also adhere to strict conduct guidelines that protect freelancers from unfair treatment and demands. Furthermore, these platforms typically have an algorithm that dictates when a project should be due depending on the complexity so that the freelancer has enough time to do their best work without a client making unfair demands of when it should be delivered.

There are several more advantages to these types of sites, which is why chapter three recommends this option as the best alternative for freelancers who do not yet have much experience working in their niche. Freelancers get to work under the supportive supervision of professionals who provide you with the chance to build a robust portfolio and with tips on how to create an attractive profile that will get clients interested.

The downside to these types of platforms is that often they require that all communication be centralized within their site, not allowing freelancers to get in touch with clients by any means other than the platform.

Another potential drawback is that most of the work you do on these sites is not allowed to be shared anywhere else other than on their site, which limits how much you can work to grow your own personal brand or agency if that is what you decide to do moving forward.

Job boards do not require that you do anything other on their website other than update your profile and look through available projects to get started. While this business model provides freelancers with the freedom to market their own brand and communicate with clients outside of work, there is no support or supervision which can lead to clients taking advantage of a freelancer.

Typically, a client has the ability to post a project without having to adhere to any specifications about how they are allowed to communicate with a client. Job boards do not limit how many revisions a client can request, how much they can charge, or even when they need to pay a client after a project has been completed. Another issue is communication control. Job boards do not protect clients from unfair communication or treatment, which is something that can be very demotivating to a freelancer who is just getting started. For this reason, chapter three recommends that job boards be used by more experienced freelancers who know how to manage client relations and know how to detect when a project is not fairly set up.

Furthermore, if you have been working for a full year as a freelancer without any significant breaks during that period, you can begin to start using both options as opposed to sticking to just one. It is better to begin your freelancing journey by opting for just one method as opposed to trying to find work both on freelance platforms and job boards. Trying to combine both will ultimately lead your performance to falter in both since you will struggle to handle the workload from both and try to remember the different specifics of what each platform requires you to do in terms of client interactions. For example, if you are working in a freelance platform but have also taken on a project you saw posted in a job board, you will struggle to remember which clients you are not allowed to contact outside the website. Trying to handle projects from both websites might lead you to get in touch with a client outside of the freelance platform where you are collaborating with them and make you lose the client due to not adhering to the guidelines.

The Importance of Getting Started

The conclusion has summarized the most fundamental considerations expressed in the chapters of this book to remind you of them as you begin your journey toward professional autonomy. There is not much else left to say other than thank you for investing your time and energy into ensuring that your first step is as well-positioned and purposeful as you can make it. The world of freelancing is expanding now more than ever before, but what you make of this opportunity will be unlike what anyone before you has ever done.

Freelancing is not a destination, it is a way of life. There will be times that are very challenging, but through those challenges, you will learn how to overcome any obstacle by coming to life prepared and ready to take every experience as a learning opportunity.

Your ability to harness your unique talents and experiences to manifest a life that is unlike you have ever lived before will be the light you must always follow through the struggles of this venture. Regardless of how well-prepared you are, there will always be challenges along the way. However, as this book has explained, the idea is not to eschew difficulty but to know how to meet it with a well-informed mind and a resilient spirit.

By reading this book, you have taken the first and most important step to creating the life you envision for yourself. Do not forget that you have the ability to make your aspirations a reality for you and your dependents. Now the only thing left to do is to get started and never give up.

Good luck, you will do great.

If you enjoyed this book and found it useful on your personal journey to becoming a successful freelancer, please leave a positive review online to help others find it and use it on their own path.

Before you go, we just wanted to say thank you for purchasing our book. You could have picked from dozens of other books on the same topic but you took a chance and chose this one. So, a HUGE thanks to you for getting this book and for reading all the way to the end.

Now, we wanted to ask you for a small favor. COULD YOU PLEASE CONSIDER POSTING A REVIEW ON THE PLATFORM? (Reviews are one of the easiest ways to support the work of independent authors.)

This feedback will help us continue to write the type of books that will help you get the results you want. So if you enjoyed it, please let us know!

We wish you much Success on your Journey!